Aratus Cilix

Ptolemeus Aegyptius

M. Manlius Romanus

Azophi Arabus

MILLENNIUM PROPHECIES

MILLENNIUM PROPHECIES

PREDICTIONS FOR THE

Year 2000

and Beyond

FROM THE WORLD'S
GREATEST SEERS
AND MYSTICS

Stephen Skinner

CARLTON

THIS IS A CARLTON BOOK

This edition published by Carlton Books Limited 1994

10 9 8 7 6 5 4 3 2 1

ISBN 1-85868-034-4

Design: Steve Wilson
Project art direction: Bobbie Colgate-Stone and Fiona Knowles
Project editor: Tessa Rose
Picture research: Sharon Hutton
Production: Sarah Schuman

Printed and bound in Italy

CONTENTS

INTRODUCTION

What does the immediate future hold for us all? The end of the millennium is due in less than seven years. Who can afford to ignore the momentous events promised for this time?

An early 16th-century vision of Christ presiding over the Resurrection of the dead

The end of the world has always had a grim fascination for prophets, and perhaps even more so for their readers or listeners. We envisage it in terms of either natural disaster afflicting us (like earthquake, famine, plague, flood, fire, freezing, cosmic collision, ecological catastrophe), or a divine being punishing us for wrongs committed.

Whichever of these may overtake us, it is inconceivable that the world will end: we, mankind, may come to a full-stop, but it, the Earth, will continue to hurtle round the sun just as it always has. But will it?

Huge cosmic collisions between earth and forces from outer space have been recorded in the sacred writings of every race. Some modern prophets, like Immanuel Velikovsky, have drawn on this ancient evidence to suggest that the time may be ripe for another such planetary collision. It would take only one meteorite of modest size to capsize the climate of the planet. At a stroke we Earth-dwellers could be wiped out as surely as the occupants of Atlantis were once allegedly destroyed.

For the prophet, whether a bearded high priest or a bearded hippy, the fascination of pinpointing the last apocalyptic day is overwhelming. To do this, the prophet looks at the wheels of the cosmic clock to understand the nature of time. He or she measures the ages, probes back to find the date of creation, and performs mental gymnastics on every single number mentioned in the Bible or other holy books, scans the skies, or tries to find a mighty enough planetary conjunction which could just trigger the fatal event.

All the worry about nihilation and eternal damnation might prove to be misplaced, however. The gaping jaws of the Apocalypse might not snap shut, ensnaring us all. Many might survive the ordeal, or it might never happen because there is no need for it. Even now the children of the Sixties, that time of hope and idealism, are taking up the reins of power. Guided by their vision for a better world, we might avoid the worst scenario. The New Age philosophers and their forerunners, like Aleister Crowley and Madame Blavatsky, have wedged open the doors of perception to a wider consciousness based on non-materialistic values. Their influence may just prevent mankind from self-

The four terrible horsemen of the Apocalypse

destructing and lead him to a paradise on earth in the form of a theocratic kingdom which can look forward to a thousand years of peace.

Despite the fact that we are all still here, and many a deadline solemnly proclaimed has passed without so much as an apocalyptic tremor, we should not dismiss the positive effects of such seemingly negative predictions. There is nothing like a deadline to galvanize humanity to action, or greater piety — or even greater craziness. Prophets act as our collective conscience — they keep us on our toes. We may not always believe that the end is nigh, but perhaps it would be better for us sometimes if we acted as though it were.

Even if the world survives the magic 2000 years after the birth of Christ, or 2160 years since the beginning of the Piscean Age, or the next grand conjunction, or avoids the destruction of its protective atmosphere, or any of the other cyclical deadlines looming up thick and fast, one thing is certain — every person reading this book will in less than a century from now meet his or her own end of the world.

If this book does nothing but stir its readers into making preparations for that day, by doing now what they might otherwise have put off, then its author will be satisfied with his handiwork.

CARPE DIEM

Stephen Skinner

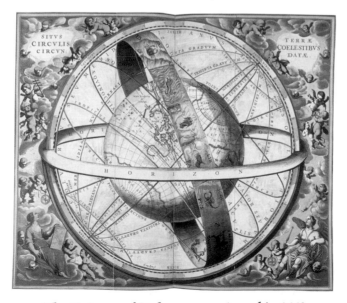

The Universe of Ptolemy, as envisaged in 1660

The ANCIENT WORLD

The Ancients knew much about the measurement of long periods of time. With Apollo's help the Greek prophetesses could look deep into the future. Unimaginably long periods of time have been measured between the birth and the destruction of the Universe: are we nearing the end of this period?

Time and Chronology

We need to examine the concept and meaning of time in order to determine when to expect the Apocalypse.

Time is what distinguishes the present moment from the domain of prophecy and the domain of history. We can only truly experience that infinitesimal sliver of time that is called the present. The past we can experience only vicariously, through memory or history. A very few people – true prophets – do seem to be able to perceive glimpses of the future. To map what they discover, we need to understand chronology.

Chronology, the science of computing time both for daily and historical periods, differs from history in that it takes no account of the significance of events or their relationship to each other. Many early civilizations used as their timepiece the changes in the moon's shape over the lunar month. This was soon found to be unsatisfactory, however, because it could not be used to measure the seasons, especially the growing seasons on which lives and livelihoods depended. Seasons wax and wane depending upon the earth's revolution round the Sun – not an easy phenomenon to measure with the naked eye.

More advanced civilizations used the solar year, and dated events from some arbitrary date of national

The beginning of the Muslim era

importance, such as the beginning of a king's reign. The Greeks employed this "epochal" method of dating. They used the Olympic Games to break their chronology into groups of four years, dating events from the victory of Coroebus in the first Olympic Games of 776 BC. This system was first suggested by Timaeus around 260 BC. If the Greeks' Olympic system were still in use today, AD 1994 would be the year of the Greek Olympiad 2771, and AD 2000 would be the year of the Greek Olympiad 2777.

The Babylonians chose the date of the foundation of their kingdom, 26 February 747 BC, under Nabonasser as their base line for calculating dates. This in turn was used by the famous Alexandrian astronomer and "father of astrology", Ptolemy, who flourished in Egypt in the second century AD.

Similar thinking lay behind the dating system used by the Romans, which starts from the foundation of the city of Rome, somewhere between 747 BC and 753 BC. For the Romans, AD 2000 would be 2754 AUC, *anno urbis conditae*, meaning from the founding of the city.

Islam dates its epoch from the retreat of the prophet Mohammed from Mecca to Medina on 16 July AD 622. The year 1378 in the Islamic calendar is the equivalent of the Gregorian AD 2000.

The key date in Christian countries is, of course, the birth of Christ. Even this concept of BC (before Christ) and AD (*anno domini*, or after Christ's birth), was not actually put into practice until the monk Dionysius Exiguus suggested it in AD 533. Before his idea was adopted, Christian countries used a dating system based on the supposed beginning of the world, or *anno mundi*. The Irish Protestant prelate and scholar Archbishop Ussher (1581–1656) was responsible for the assumption that the world began and man was created in 4004 – some 5,502 or 5,508 or even 6,000 years (according to the Septuagint, the Greek version of the Bible) before Christ's birth.

Modern geological techniques have shown these dates to be ludicrously inaccurate. However, despite this shortcoming, they do at least deal with a time-scale in human history that we are able to relate to – just imagine trying to encompass a dating system that spanned 4,600,000,000 years to the present!

These notional dates of when the world began, or Christ was born, or Rome was founded are symptoms of man's need to mould reality to his own pattern of thinking. Days, lunar months and years do not, in fact, fit neatly together as exact multiples, but because we prefer a "tidy" chronology we have invented one that appears to fit together.

Epochs and even numbers hold enormous fascination for us. Hence 1000 years or 2000 years after the birth of Christ suddenly become important points in the history of mankind. This is why chronology is a key to prophecy; to find out what the future holds for us, you must first of all know where you stand in the procession of events that together make up human history. Certainly, the next seven years mark the culmination point of many key dates.

If you are guided by Archbishop Ussher's dating method, the key date will be 1995, exactly 6000 years on from the "beginning" of the world. Alternatively, perhaps 1999 is the key date, for if you count from 5502 (another world "birth date") this year marks the 7500th birthday of the world or indeed the universe.

For contemporary astrological speculator Richard W. Noone, the key date is 5 May 2000. For Christians, however, the key date is still Christmas 2000. I did not, you will note, state 25 December 2000, because it is doubtful whether this was indeed the day on which Christ was born.

Ptolemy, father of astrology

THE SOLAR SYSTEM'S CLOCK

Time is recorded astronomically, by the great clock of the solar system and its setting in the universe. The most basic cosmic occurrence for man is the rotation of the earth on its own axis, which defines the length of a 24-hour day.

The rotation of the Earth round the Sun defines a year, and the rotation of the moon round the Earth a lunar month or, imperfectly, a calendar month. Unfortunately, the creator did not make these three basic natural cycles divisible one into another. There are not, for example, an even number of days in the year or in the lunar month. As a result, man has produced several systems of reckoning drawn from his imagination. Perhaps the neatest of these was the Egyptian year of 360 days made up of 12 months, each of 30 days, with five (or occasionally six) days dedicated to the gods as holy days.

When Julius Caesar reformed the Roman calendar in 46 BC, 1 January was chosen as the date to mark the beginning of the year. In England in AD 1155 this was changed to 25 March, to coincide roughly with the

Ussher named the date of creation

Spring Equinox, and in conformity with European custom. In 1582 Pope Gregory XIII reformed the Julian calendar; 1 January was again adopted as the first day of the year, but the practice of each centennial year counting as a leap year was dropped. England did not realign itself with Europe until 1752, by which time the Julian calendar was 11 days out of step with the seasons.

Meaning of the Millennium

'Millennium' is a Latin word which simply means a period of one thousand years. However, this timespan, equalling about forty generations, has come to have a special meaning in the religions of Judaism and Christianity.

St John sees the end of the millennium

The Adoration of the Magi heralded two millenniums of Christianity

One thousand years was the period for which Satan was supposed to be bound, and also the duration of Christ's absence from Earth. The early Christians thought that Christ's second coming would occur within their lifetime. The disappointment of this expectation led to a revision of the timescale and the belief in his return after 1000 years.

The year 999 saw extensive preparation across Europe for Christ's return. When He failed to materialize, hopes were then pinned on a succession of dates until the year 2000 was finally settled upon. Even in these relatively godless times, millions of people are awaiting with bated breath the second millennium after Christ's birth.

American fundamentalist Christians form the vanguard of the expectant. His arrival, they believe, will be heralded by specific "signs", notably devastating wars and natural disasters, followed by a period of rule by the Antichrist. After mankind has endured these trials Christ will return to judge both the living and the dead, set up his kingdom, and rule it for a further 1000 years. Sometimes the actual period of His rule, a time of perfect happiness for those who passed judgement, is referred to as the millennium.

The term Apocalypse is derived from Greek and literally means "to uncover". The term can also mean a revelation, as in something revealed by God to a chosen prophet; for example, the Apocalypse of St John the Divine, the last book of the Bible. There are also a number of other apocalypses, supposedly revelations of the end-time or future state of the world, written by Hellenized Jews and early Christians in the form of visions. The branch of theology concerned with beliefs about the end of time is called eschatology. The four most important events in this category for Christians are the second coming of Christ, the resurrection of the dead, the last judgement, and the final recompense.

Belief in the importance of the millennial year AD 2000 is grounded in the sacred Jewish and Christian texts. Visionary thought concerning the end of this millennium comes from books written and visions seen between the middle of the second century BC and the end of the first century AD. These may have derived some of their inspiration from other cultures; early Persian mysticism, for example, contains strong apocalyptic elements, and in the broadest sense of eschatological or end-time beliefs, so do Ugaritic, Akkadian, Babylonian, Egyptian, Cannoned, Greek and Latin works.

Hesiod, a Greek poet of the eighth century BC, saw history as a divinely ordered succession of periods, descending from the golden age, through the silver to the bronze and then the iron age, long before historians used these terms to date periods according to the types of metal tools in use. For Hesiod, the end-time would come with warfare and social upheavals which would lead Zeus to destroy mankind for its wickedness.

In many traditions, the day of judgement or the end of the world is often referred to as Doomsday, derived

Zeus was to destroy mankind

from the word "doom", which means "law" and by implication "punishment". The idea is that everybody gets their just deserts in the end. It does not seem to have occurred to the formulators of the systems of religious belief that the universe may not in fact be fair, and actually may have little regard for man's conceptions of doom or law.

Fixing the date for the millennium is not as easy as simply adding 2000 years to Christ's birth. For a start, no one knows when Christ was born, and the best guess is 4 BC. By this reckoning, the millennium is due to arrive in 1996.

There is a further complication in that we use one number to refer to a whole year. For example, "1996" refers not to a date but to a twelve-month period. So should we aim for the beginning, middle or end of the year?

WHEN WILL THE MILLENNIUM ARRIVE?

Calculating the start of the 21st century is not as simple as it may seem. The obvious starting point for the millennium is midnight on 31 December 1999. However, before the 21st century can be said to begin, a full 20 centuries must have ticked away since the birth of Christ. Take the year 20 AD – at the beginning of this year only 19 years had passed.

Similarly, at the beginning of the year 2000 only 1999 years will have passed. The true arithmetical millennium, therefore, will come on midnight 31 December 2000, one year after the date many people are pinning their hopes on. So the question is, do you follow the arithmetic strictly, or simply go for the first moment of that magic number, the year 2000?

Further, if you are measuring from Christ's birth, do you take 4 BC or the first moment of AD 1? Do you use 25 December or one of the other proposed birthdays? Anyway, there is always the chance of the millennium coming late!

In this book we have taken the simplistic view and assumed that the millennium will begin on 1 January AD 2000, but the reader is free to make the above adjustments as he or she sees fit.

Furnaces and Fire Worshippers

The Book of Daniel is one of the most controversial books of the Old Testament and probably the most important book of Old Testament prophecy, filled with key numbers.

The Judgement of Daniel on the attempted seduction of Susanna

The Book of Daniel is reckoned to be the earliest canonical book of prophecy, compiled c. 580 BC. Some scholars prefer to date it from the second century BC, partly to account for the accuracy of its prophecies. The historical events it relates happened between 534 and 607 BC, during

which time Daniel's vision also revealed things about the end of time.

It is obvious that the Book of Daniel has been compiled from a number of sources. Whole books have been cut out of Daniel because they were thought to be non-canonical, that is, not part of accepted scripture; among

these "rogues" are The History of Susanna, about an attempted seduction, and Bel and the Dragon.

The Book of Daniel opens "in the third year of the reign of Jehoiakim king of Judah", after Nebuchadnezzar, King of Babylon, had conquered Jerusalem and taken the Jewish people into slavery. The best of their children were taken to Babylon to learn the Chaldean ways. Four children were selected and given Chaldean names to replace their Hebrew ones. Daniel was among those shown special favour and renamed Belteshazzar. For religious reasons, Daniel and his three companions asked for a water and vegetarian diet rather than the standard meat and wine rations.

At the end of three years Daniel "had understanding in all visions and dreams". Nebuchadnezzar called for the children and found that not only did they have "fairer countenances", due to the vegetarian diet, but they also had a greater skill, wisdom and understanding of magic than his own Chaldean astrologers. Daniel rapidly proves himself the equal of Nebuchadnezzar's magicians and sorcerers, just as Aaron had defeated Pharaoh's magicians. It seems that in every age the best prophets were also the best magicians, and Jewish.

In 8:14 Daniel is told that the sanctuary and the host will be trodden under foot "unto 2300 days" and "at the time of the end shall be the vision".

In 9:2 Daniel states that "the Lord . . .would accomplish seventy years in the desolations of Jerusalem". Seventy years is, of course, 25,550 days, the approximate period (in years) of the precession of the Zodiac.

In 9:26 Daniel is told to "know therefore and understand that from the going forth of the commandment to restore and to build [again] Jerusalem unto the Messiah the Prince shall be seven weeks, and threescore and two weeks". This commandment was issued by Artaxerxes in 457 BC. Now, 7 + 62 weeks equals 483 "days", or the 483 years from 457 BC until the crucifixion of Christ in AD 30, taking into account the four-year calendar correction of 46 BC. So Daniel has correctly prophesied Christ's advent as the "Messiah the Prince".

The prophecy continues "after threescore and two weeks shall the Messiah be cut off [crucified], but not for himself: and [they shall be no more the Messiah's people]", implying the Jews' rejection of Jesus's claim to be the Messiah.

The destruction of the Temple of Jerusalem is then prophesied: "and the people of the prince that shall come shall destroy the city and the sanctuary" (9:26). This took place in 70 AD, which is suggested by the reference to one week seven days, in which "he shall confirm the covenant with many

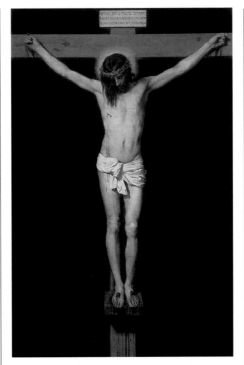

Daniel told of a Messiah's crucifixion

for one week: and in the midst of the week he shall cause the sacrifice and the oblation to cease".

In the last chapter Daniel asks "How long shall it be to the end of these wonders" (12:6). The inscrutable answer he receives is "it shall be for a time, times, and a half". Daniel, like us, complains "I heard, but I understand not". Two last numbers are supplied as

boundary dates of the final apocalyptic events, "there shall be 1290 days. Blessed is he that waiteth, and cometh to the 1335 days. But go thy way till the end".

How should we reconcile these conflicting dates? It could be that after the destruction of the Temple in AD 70 there were 1290 "days" times one and a half ("time, and a half")? This would yield 1935 + 70, a beginning of apocalyptic events in 2005 AD.

Then "the end therefore shall be with a flood, and unto the end of the war desolations are determined." At this time the Archangel Michael, who protects Israel in time of trouble, will arise. The dead – "them that sleep in the dust of the earth" – shall awake; some, but not all, will be resurrected and granted immortality: they will shine like stars in the firmament. The less fortunate, for their part, will be condemned to everlasting shame and contempt.

Using the same logic on 1335, the final resurrection of the dead should take place halfway through the year AD 2072, when the blessed who have waited will ascend to the stars.

GOD'S CALCULATOR: KEY NUMBERS IN THE BOOK OF DANIEL

The book of Daniel is a veritable mine of numbers with which to construct possible dates for the Apocalypse. General principles of such manipulation includes reading "year" for "day", a procedure endorsed by Ezekiel (4:6). The key numbers are: Time, times and half a time – either a factor of 1.5, or sometimes 3.5 years; this is also expressed as season, seasons and half a season. Two thousand three hundred evenings and mornings, possibly representing 2300 years. It is a key phrase for the Seventh Day Adventists . Seventy weeks, also 7 weeks, 62 weeks, and 1 week, making respectively 490, 49, 434 and 7 years. One thousand two hundred and ninety days and 1335 days times 1.5 for the dating of the Apocalypse. Daniel mourned for three whole weeks (10:2), by which a period of tribulations of 21 years may in fact be meant.

Chariots of Fire

*Did Ezekiel really see God's arrival in a chariot
accompanied by cherubim, or was he simply tripping?*

Ezekiel's vision of Jehovah and the four cherubim

The date of the Book of the prophet Ezekiel is often put at 595–7 BC. The brief apocalypse incorporated in the Book dates from the same time of crisis in Jewish history as that depicted in the Book of Daniel. This crisis was precipitated by the attacks of the Babylonian king, Nebuchadnezzar. In the course of his war with the Egyptians, he captured Jerusalem and took back with him as hostages King Jehoiakim and his court. Ezekiel was a Jewish priest and prophet during this period of history.

The first chapter of Ezekiel, specifically verses 4 to 28, contains one of the most extraordinary descriptions of a vision ever written. What Ezekiel saw has been the subject of millions of words and many pictures, but in essence it was this:

A great whirlwind containing a very bright amber fire came from the north to the river Chebar, where Ezekiel was sitting. In the middle of this brightness were four creatures called cherubim. These beings had some of the physical characteristics of men (their hands, for example, were shaped like human hands), but only one of them had a human face – the others bore, respectively, the faces of a lion, ox and eagle, like the beasts of the Apocalypse of St John hundreds of years later. Each cherubim also had four long wings, two touching above their heads and two folded around their bodies, and above their heads were crystal halos like the night sky. Their feet were like a calf's and gleamed like brass. These beings looked more like the winged bulls of ancient Babylon than the Victorian conception of angels. Almost 700 years later St John, after he had swallowed the same substance, saw the same cherubim. Can we expect a similar visitation in the next few years?

The cherubim moved very rapidly backwards and forwards without moving their wings, making a sound like rushing water or a large crowd. They were accompanied by something resembling ball lightning and beryl-coloured wheels within wheels, like gyroscopes, which were full of bright eyes and did not turn as they moved. The cherubims flashed like lightning as they moved, and folded their wings downwards when they were still. Above the heads of the cherubim was a sapphire throne containing a fiery god who looked like an old man, surrounded by a multicoloured rainbow of splendour.

Without a doubt, such a detailed description is intended to make one believe that Ezekiel did actually witness this incredible scene. There is no attempt to describe the event in obscure, symbolic terms. Ezekiel really saw something fantastic. But was this extraordinary phenomenon one of the "chariots of the gods", a sort of early UFO, to use Erich von Daniken's phrase, or the arrival of some god, perhaps Jehovah himself?

Jehovah commands Ezekiel to get up from his prone position, and gives him instructions with regard to the Jews who were in exile. In true prophetic style, Jehovah outlines a number of punishments to be served out to Ezekiel's fellow countrymen for their hardheartedness and interest in idols. Ezekiel, however, is a reluctant bearer of bad tidings and much more at home as a visionary, so Jehovah has to provide some convincing arguments

before he will agree to go back and threaten the people of Israel over their unacceptable conduct (3:17–22).

At the end of their conversation, the visitor takes off into the ether, or, as Ezekiel puts it: "I heard also the noise of the wings of the living creatures that touched one another, and the noise of the wheels over against them, and noise of a great rushing. So the spirit lifted me up, and took me away . . ." (3:13-14). The temptation to ascribe these sounds to some advanced flying machine is almost overwhelming. It seems too palpable to have just been an internal vision.

If Christ returns to Earth at the millennium, for the second time, will He make a similarly spectacular entrance? Probably not is the answer. Jehovah was always much more of a showman than Christ. However, as next time Christ is due to arrive for the execution of the Last Judgement, perhaps He will adopt some of the fire and fury of His father, Jehovah.

PSYCHEDELIC VISIONS

Ezekiel's description of the arrival of Jehovah has the immediacy of a psychedelic vision, and even from our perspective, 2,500 years after the event, it is arresting. The idea that the prophet's vision may well have been drug-induced is not as outrageous as it seems. Consider these words by Ezekiel, "an hand was sent unto me; and lo, a roll of a book was therein . . . moreover he said unto me . . . eat this roll" (2:9–3:1). Ezekiel did as he was told, "so I opened my mouth, and . . . did eat it". This substance was at once provided by his vision and helped to fuel it. It was a sort of sacrament, which was also a book with writing in it.

St John, as recorded in his Apocalypse almost 700 years later, was also told to eat a little book: "Give me the little book. And he said unto me, Take it, and eat it up; and it shall make thy belly bitter, but it shall be in thy mouth sweet as honey" (10:9).

If you think that in either of these instances a symbolic "eating" was meant, the words of Ezekiel refute the idea: he was to "cause thy belly to eat, and fill thy bowels with this roll that I give thee" (3:2–3). You can hardly get more anatomically specific than this!

Ezekiel and St John ingested something during the course of their visions which enabled them to see other dimensions, other times, and perhaps even the end of the world.

Jehovah's Throne seen by Ezekiel

Persecution and Prophecies

Prophets were often less than welcome in their own countries. Perhaps the most universally disliked and persecuted Hebrew prophet was Jeremiah.

Jeremiah's first book of prophecies was cut to pieces and then burnt by his fellow-countrymen. He was often imprisoned under very unpleasant conditions for his apparently unpatriotic prophecies, and finished up attaching himself to the Babylonian governor for his own safety before fleeing to Egypt, where he was finally stoned to death for his lugubrious insights.

Many prophets seem to have had their vocation forced upon them rather than actively seeking it. Apart from the well-known prophets like Jeremiah there seem to have been bands of roving prophets as part of everyday life in ancient Israel, not necessarily all of them Jewish. Some in fact may have even been Philistine. For example, in Samuel 10:5 Saul is told:

"After that thou shalt come to the hill of God, where is the garrison of the Philistines: and it shall come to pass, when thou art come thither to the city, that thou shalt meet a company of prophets coming down from the high place with a psaltery, and a tabret, and a pipe, and a harp, before them; and they shall prophesy; and the Spirit of the Lord will come upon thee, and thou shalt prophesy with them, and shalt be turned into another man."

It seems as if Saul was incidentally initiated into the mysteries of prophecy in the company of these wandering Philistine prophets. The narrative continues with Saul's kinsmen being very surprised at his new-found prophetic talents.

One of the ongoing promises of the prophets has always been the arrival of a Messiah who will save the Jewish nation from whatever persecutors they happen to have at the time. The Jews looked forward, and still do, to the coming of a saviour, one born to the royal line of the house of David. Christ did not deliver them from the Romans, and was consequently dismissed by most Jews as a pseudo-Messiah.

For reasons which seem to be buried deep in the Jewish psyche, these periods of enslavement have always provoked the idea that they were a punishment for neglecting their god. This reaction is an extreme version of the almost universal religious idea that the world is ruled by a god or gods who dispense justice.

Having said this, the Jewish reaction, above that of all other religions, was to produce a series of prophets whose hallmarks were a warning against past misbehaviour as

Jeremiah, the gloomiest of the Hebrew prophets, by Michelangelo

an explanation of present misfortune, and a promise of future bliss if their rules are adhered to. The repeated degradation and enslavement to pagan nations endured by the Jewish people and the resultant intense desire for the fulfilment of age-old prophecies of ultimate glory gave rise to a wealth of Jewish apocalyptic literature, and a strong expectation of the arrival or return of the Messiah.

The idea of a coming Messiah was a Christian inheritance from Judaism. Christianity, of course, maintained that the Messiah had arrived, and had shown Himself several times after the crucifixion to His disciples. The common belief was that He would soon return yet again, hence the concept of the Second Coming.

Many believed that He would return with an army, maybe even an army of angels, and triumph as a military saviour over their oppressors, the Romans. Early belief, before it was mythologized by Origen and St Augustine, was clearly in an earthly kingdom of God, not in some long-deferred heaven. But as the centuries rolled on the expectation was moved forward and hopes were pinned on years like AD 1000 or AD 2000.

From a purely military point of view, Egypt, then Babylon (the Persians) and, finally, the Romans were the main enemies of Israel and its smaller sister kingdom of Judah. Christian commentators have ceased to look at the historical perspective and often take the names of these countries as symbols of evil. Even the later Protestant view of Catholicism, with its headquarters in Rome, shares the feelings that the Jews of ancient Israel

The last days and ominous Fall of Babylon

had for the conquering Roman armies, who eventually destroyed their Temple in AD 70.

The result of this is that apocalyptic writings, both Jewish and Christian, often speak of the destruction of Babylon (or in a more guarded way of the destruction of Rome), and the arrival of a saviour Messiah who, after a period of tribulations, will do physical battle with the enemies of the godly, often at Armageddon, before establishing a 1000-year kingdom here on earth. That, in a nutshell, is what is due to happen when the Apocalypse finally arrives.

JEWISH MYSTICAL AEONS

The Great Jubilee of 7000 years is a recurring theme in Jewish apocalyptic writings. (A full period of cosmic development is reckoned as seven times seven thousand years.) In the fifty-thousandth year the universe is expected to return to its source. This was first expounded in the book Temunah, written around AD 1250 and based on a new interpretation of the "Shemittah" or Aeon.

The current 7000-year period is one of judgement, with its attendant commandments and prohibitions, and opposition between pure and impure, holy and unholy.

In the Aeon due at the end of this century, the next Shemittah, the law or Torah will no longer contain prohibitions, the power of evil will be curbed and Utopia will be realized, like the 1000-year reign of the Messiah. This idea is very like that of the 12th-century Calabrian Christian visionary Joachim of Fiore, which outlined three cosmic periods – those of the Father, the Son and the Holy Spirit.

The Greek Prophetesses

Prophecy is not the exclusive province of Old Testament prophets. The Greek words for prophetic power are "manteia" and "propheteia".

The word "prophetes" means "a person who speaks for someone else", which is exactly what a prophet does in speaking for a god.

The ancient Greeks consulted the will of the gods on all important occasions of public and private life, such as the sale of slaves, cultivation of a field, marriages, voyages, loans and so on.

The oracle was not merely a revelation to satisfy the curiosity of man, but a sanction or authorization by the deity for what was intended.

Cassandra, daughter of King Priam, was given the gift of prophecy by the god of the sun, Apollo. In vain she foretold the fall of Troy, in which she was captured and ravished by Ajax,

but no one believed her until it was too late and the prophecy had come true.

Apart from those given the gift of prophecy by the gods themselves, there were also trained priestesses of Apollo, called Pythia or Sibyls. The most famous of the Sibyls was the Cumaean Sibyl, who is reputed to have guided Aeneas on his journey through the underworld. The entrance to this underworld was near Baia on the Bay of Naples, in Italy (and still exists). An oracle book purporting to contain the sayings of these Sibyls, called *The Sibylline Oracles*, was very popular in the Middle Ages.

The most celebrated of all oracles was the oracle of Apollo at Delphi whose name was Pytho. The word Pytho means to consult as well as "to putrify", a reference to the fumes which arose from a cleft in the earth at Delphi and which were sometimes said to be the stench from the corpse of the dead serpent that once inhabited the chasm. These fumes intoxicated the priestess, who uttered the god's warnings in a trance. It is possible that the fumes acted as a hallucinogenic. In the inner sanctuary, the priestess sat on a high golden tripod (a three-legged chair) above the cleft from which issued the conscious-altering fumes, in front of a golden statue of Apollo, the sun god. An eternal fire fed with resinous fir wood blazed in front of the statue. The inner roof of the temple was covered with laurel garlands and upon the altar laurel was burnt as an incense – a heady mixture indeed.

In response to a question put to her the priestess would rapidly enter a state of delirious intoxication, uttering a stream of words, moans, and sounds

Cassandra foretold her rape and the calamitous siege and fall of Troy

The Delphic Sibyl, prophetess of Apollo

which one of the five priests or "prophetes" would write down and later interpret. These interpretations were often presented in verse in the form of hexameters. Sometimes the effect of the smoke upon the priestess was so great that she leapt or fell from the tripod, fell into convulsions, and sometimes died. For this reason, in later times three priestesses were kept on standby.

Those who consulted the oracle had to wear laurel-garlands tied with virgin wool, to pay a fee, and then sacrifice a goat, ox or sheep, which had to be a perfect, healthy specimen.

The divine agency in Pytho was first discovered by shepherds whose sheep fell into convulsions when they approached the chasm over which the temple was later built. People from all over the ancient world flocked to consult this oracle, not just from Greece. It did not lose its power until the sanctuary was done away with by the

Christian Emperor Theodosius in the 4th century AD.

There were at least 20 other well-known oracles in the Greek world, of which the most interesting to us is the oracle of Apollo at Didyma, usually called the oracle of the Branchidae, in the territory of Miletus. This was the oracle usually consulted by the Ionians and Aeolians. The altar itself was said to have been constructed by Heracles, and the temple by Branchus, a son of Apollo, who had come as a priest from the oracle at Delphi.

The cult relied upon the mediumship of inspired priestesses, and the techniques employed to obtain their divine intoxication were described by the Greek Iamblichus of Chalcis, who died in about AD 335:

"The prophetess of Branchus either sits upon a pillar, or holds in her hand a rod bestowed by some deity, or moistens her feet or the hem of her garment with water . . . and by these means . . . she prophesies."

Another passage in the same ancient text mentions the use of a bronze tripod in a rite of prophecy. This oracle is of particular interest to us because it used the techniques of prophecy which were later borrowed by Nostradamus, who in 1555 used them to discover the darkest secrets of the millennium and the events leading up to the year 2000 (see panel).

NOSTRADAMUS BORROWS FROM THE ANCIENT GREEKS

Nostradamus describes his prophetic technique in Century I, Quatrain 1 and 2:

"Sitting alone at night in secret study, Rested on a brazen tripod . . .
The hand-held wand is placed in the midst of the BRANCHES,
He moistens with water his foot and garment's hem,
Fear and a Voice make him quake in his sleeves,
Divine splendour, the divine sits nigh."

Here, Nostradamus is describing the divinatory rite of Branchus. The word BRANCHES was in capital letters in the original printing, a clear hint that it was intended to be understood in more than one way. Nostradamus was almost certainly using the word to refer to the secret techniques of Branchus and the Greek oracle at Didyma which inspired his gift of prophecy.

It is likely that Nostradamus became acquainted with this work early in his life, as there is reason to believe that copies of a translation were circulating among French students of mysticism as early as 1500. It was republished in France in the 1540s, and it may be significant that Nostradamus began to issue his almanacs not long after that event. Certainly, it is likely that he employed similar methods to those described in the book combined with astrology as his method of obtaining his amazingly accurate knowledge of the future.

CLOCKS
of
STONE

The reason for the construction of the
Great Pyramid at Giza has been lost
in the mists of history. For the Victorians
it became the centre of enormous
prophetic activity: they felt the world
was about to pass through the last portal
into the King's Chamber, heralding the
end of time.

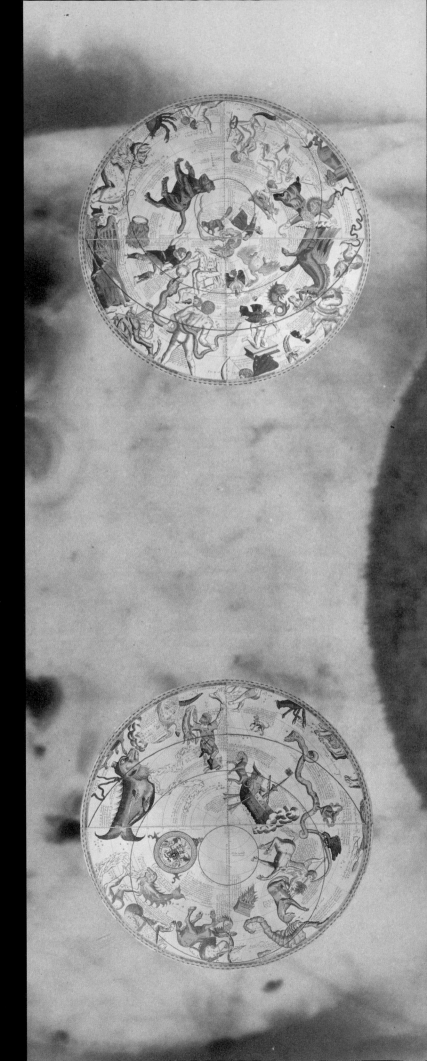

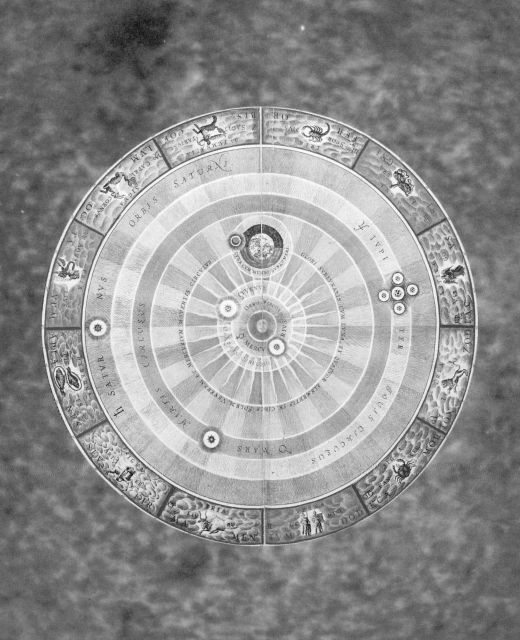

The Horoscope for AD 2000

Astrology can help us to take the pulse of the future. Among the pivotal dates looming on our horizon, that of 18 August 1999 is one of the most widely known.

This date was given prominence by Professor Hideo Itokawa, the pioneer of Japan's rocket technology, in his book and in a documentary made for television in 1980.

If we examine the astrological configuration for the first minute of this date, we find Sun, Mercury and Venus in the zodiacal sign Leo, the Lion with the Moon and Mars in Scorpio, the Eagle with Pluto closely alongside in Sagittarius, Jupiter and Saturn in Taurus, the Bull with Uranus and Neptune in Aquarius, the Water Bearer. The four signs in which the planets are quartered are the four beasts of the Apocalypse of St John, the four heads of the cherubim of Ezekiel, and the four symbols on the last card of the tarot pack, the World. They are symbols for the so-called "four last things".

Professor Itokawa and his team of like-minded pessimistic futurologists were so fascinated by this so-called Grand Cross formed by the planets that he predicted widespread environmental devastation caused by conflict over energy and food resources. What the professor may have overlooked, however, is that very close to his Grand Cross – one week before it in fact, on 11 August 1999 – there will be an eclipse, the last eclipse of the 20th century. It is tempting to surmise that this eclipse will act as the catalyst and release the destructive energies of the Grand Cross.

In March 1993 we had a foretaste of what this Grand Cross holds in store for us with the conjunction of Neptune and Uranus, an extremely rare phenomenon which only occurs once in every 171 years. In the United States the conjunction was accompanied by "the single biggest blizzard storm this century", which swept from Florida to Maine, releasing more snow, hail, rain and sleet than any other similar phenomenon since 1888. It was followed by catastrophic flooding in the region of the Mississippi. The extraordinary weather that afflicted large parts of the States in 1993 may be put down to the imperfect motion of these planets.

It is not a coincidence that Neptune, or Poseidon, was the god of water,

As the stars pivot in the sky we draw nearer to the Great Conjunction of May 2000

particularly rivers and seas. His wife, Amphitrite, held sway over the sea as well as winds and earthquakes – we may well hear from her again before the end of the century.

Another extremely rare configuration involving all the planets, and one which has been misrepresented as a Grand Cross by some writers, will be formed on 4 May 2000 at exactly 3.12am Greenwich Mean Time. On this day the Earth will find itself in opposition to the planets, at 13 degrees 58 minutes of Scorpio, with only distant Pluto, at 11 degrees 21 minutes of Sagittarius, providing any gravitational muscle against the rest.

This mighty conjunction of planets will not be observable to the naked eye, and becomes clear in the mind only when it is plotted on paper. At right angles to the Earth, forming a "square" aspect of 90 degrees, will be the two other outer planets, Uranus and Neptune; Uranus at 17 degrees 46 minutes of Aquarius, and Neptune at 4 degrees 40 minutes of Aquarius. The inner planets of the solar system will line up as follows: Venus at 19 degrees 23 minutes of Aries; Mercury at 20 degrees 8 minutes of Aries; Moon at 13 degrees 24 minutes of Taurus; Sun at 13 degrees 58 minutes of Taurus; Jupiter at 17 degrees 31 minutes of Taurus; Saturn at 20 degrees 12 minutes of Taurus; Venus at 10 degrees 56 minutes of Gemini.

Astrologers have a compelling term for this unique configuration: "opposition". Who knows what natural disturbances might occur on Earth as a result of the gravitational pull of the entire inner solar system being pitted against us?

The Triumph of Amphitrite over the winds, seas and earthquakes

CHAOS THEORY – BUTTERFLY WINGS AND AXIAL WOBBLES

Although it could be said that the planets are too far away to have any effect on us here on Earth, you have only to examine the so-called chaos theory to realize that changes in the delicately balanced solar system may indeed be extremely significant. This theory holds that all forms of life on earth are interconnected; even the fluttering of a butterfly's wings in the Amazon can be indirectly associated with a typhoon in Hong Kong, or so the theory runs. Applying this logic, the combined gravitational pull of the other planets occupying the solar system – especially the two heaviest, Jupiter and Saturn – are not to be dismissed as irrelevant.

The line-up of such heavyweights with the Sun and the Moon could well activate sunspots, affect tides, and disturb the highly tuned crustal balance of the Earth to produce natural catastrophes such as tsunamis (tidal waves), flooding, volcanic activity and freak weather conditions.

The most extreme disaster scenario that might be produced by this configuration could involve a shift in the position of the Earth's axis. This has been demonstrated to move over time, so that the magnetic North Pole and the geographic north pole continue to drift further and further apart. Any shock to this already unstable system might cause a big "wobble".

Astrological Prophecies

A connection between astrology and the Apocalypse may seem improbable, but history shows that there has been much agreement between the casters of charts and the church authorities.

Tycho Brahe studying the planets

Through the ages prophets and astrologers alike have regarded the movements of the planets, particularly those of Saturn and Jupiter, as significant; Nostradamus, for example, used them to date future events.

The cyclical nature of the revolution of the planets led early astrologers to assume that all life, including man's life and history, was governed by cycles. These cycles might even be multiples of the time it took the outer planets to revolve round the Sun. In this period of history the two outer planets were Jupiter (taking 11.862 years) and Saturn (taking 29.458 years). It is no coincidence that the Roman god Saturn corresponds with the Greek Cronos, the god of Time and one-time ruler of the heavens.

The "Annus Magnus", or Great Year, was conceived as being the period of time it would take for the planets to return to their starting point on the first day of Creation. The return to this point would obviously be a very significant date, they reasoned. Greek philosophers like Zeno believed that the events of one age in history were repeated in another, just as human souls reincarnated.

Another Greek, the astronomer Aristarchus of Samos (c. 250 BC), who taught that the Earth moves round the Sun and who calculated the distance from the Sun to the Earth, believed that this Great Year was 2,484 ordinary years in length. Heraclitus (535–475 BC) calculated the Great Year at 10,800 years. A more valid time cycle, however, is the Precession of the Equinoxes (see panel).

In medieval Europe attempts to date the Second Coming of Christ were based on both astrological and Biblical data. The famous astronomer Tycho Brahe interpreted a new star he discovered in 1572 as a herald of the Second Coming, a view later endorsed by King James I of England. Tycho linked the star to the appearance of a great northern ruler, also mentioned by Nostradamus. This new star played a part in the millennarian speculations of Sir Christopher Heydon in 1618. Heydon prophesied the seventh return of Jupiter and Saturn "to the fiery trigon" which would bring about the destruction of the papacy, the fall of the Turks, and the return of the Jews to the new "kingdom of Christ".

The Jewish astrologer "Master Salomon" drew on astrological evidence to predict that Charles V was about to defeat the Turks, leading to the conversion of the Jews and the second coming of Christ.

A certain symmetry of dating was expected of events directly involving God. As the Flood, for example, was estimated to have occurred in 1656 Anno Mundi (ie 2348 BC), so an equally momentous upheaval, perhaps the Second Coming, was assumed for AD 1656. An additional 10 years brought commentators to the highly significant "Beast's Millennium" of 1666 AD.

The German astrologer Mussemius decided that as Christ's birth had followed a conjunction of Saturn and Jupiter in the zodiacal sign of Virgo, the Antichrist would be born when these planets met each other again on the opposite side of the zodiac in Pisces, in 1544. A later attempt to use this conjunction was made by the Bohemian astrologer Cyprian Leowitz,

Johannes Alsted, master of the cycles

who predicted the end of the world based on the conjunction of Saturn and Jupiter in 1583.

Richard Harvey predicted the world would end at noon on 28 April 1583, when Christ would appear.

Johannes Alsted, who derived some of his ideas from Tycho Brahe and the astronomer Johannes Kepler, regarded the Reformation as merely the prologue to the millennial reign of Christ. His "Speculum Mundi" is a large table on which he synchronized the three eras and seven ages of Elias with the four monarchies of Daniel and the revolutions of Saturn and Jupiter.

THE PRECESSION OF THE EQUINOXES

The key astronomical concept lying behind the theory of the cycle of the ages, or aeons, is the Precession of the Equinoxes. This astronomical phenomenon was first discovered by the ancient Egyptians. Hipparchus (c. 120 BC) found that the longitude of the stars regularly increases by 50.2 seconds of longitude every year, or, to put it another way, the apparently "fixed" belt of zodiacal stars actually moves, albeit very slowly. This is caused by the axis of the Earth describing a very gradual backwards circle as the Earth spins, a bit like a wobbly toy top.

The axis makes a complete rotation in 25,725 years (which is usually approximated to 25,600 years, or even 25,000 years). This backwards movement through the zodiacal signs means that a particular date – that of the Equinox, for example – will gradually move from one sign to another at the rate of one sign every 2,143 years. The dawning of the Age of Aquarius occurs as the polar axis leaves the sign of Pisces, where it has been for over 2,000 years, and moves backwards into Aquarius.

Horoscope for the Creation

The Pyramids and Prophecy

In 1864 Professor Piazzi Smyth, Astronomer Royal for Scotland, spent four months at Giza in Egypt trying to work out the mathematical relationships between prophecy and the dimensions of the Great Pyramid.

Professor Smyth's most astonishing observation was the accuracy with which the ratio of height to circumference of the base represents 1/2 pi. He concluded that the "sacred cubit" used by the builders of this enormous monument was the same length (25.025 imperial inches) as the one used by Moses to construct the tabernacle. With this assumption the measurements of the Great Pyramid took on a life of their own.

The oppressive passageways of the Great Pyramid are extraordinary only for the sheer weight of stone encasing them. From these few passageways the enthusiastic Christian Robert Menzies and his followers devised, or decoded, a plan which spelt out the pyramid's wider and deeper significance. Every inch of the tunnels was measured, converted into years and then matched with Biblical chronology.

The outside entrance of the pyramid was taken to represent Creation (in 4004 BC) and the Fall of Adam, the entrance of the downward sloping tunnel the Flood, and its intersection with the upward sloping tunnel the Exodus from Egypt in 1615 BC. The point at which the upward-sloping tunnel broadened into the "Grand Gallery" represented the birth of Christ, while the doorstep at its mouth symbolized Christ's life and crucifixion in AD 33.

The Victorians' certainty in Christian progress was reflected in several areas. The Grand Gallery itself was seen as the upwards progress of Christianity over 2000 years, or the "Gospel Dispensation of Grace". The King's Chamber marked the "passage into heavenly bliss of the saved". The entrance to the King's Chamber and its antechamber are of most relevance to us today, for it is this part of the pyramid which is supposed to correlate with the period of history we are now entering upon.

Morton Edgar, one of Menzies' followers, believed that the millennial age of bliss would come about in 1874. He reached this figure by taking 4128 BC as the year of Creation. Working on the assumption that Edgar was 124 years too early, and taking instead Archbishop Ussher's date of 4004 BC, the millennial age, according to the Great Pyramid, should coincide with the year 1998. Edgar also dated the end

What new chambers are hidden within these massive man-made mountains?

Sole sarcophagus in the Great Pyramid

surement. To add insult to injury, he showed that the end of the current dispensation should have come on 18 August 1882. To keep hopes alive, one Colonel J. Garnier shifted the date, gauged from the measurements marking the outer entrance to the antechamber of the King's Chamber, to 1913.

Their eagerness to fix the date of the Second Coming of Christ within their own lifetime led the Victorian millenarians to change the rule. The "inch to a year" rule gives the

following interesting set of dates. Immediately after the entrance date of 1913, 51.95 inches bring us through the opening and into the Antechamber in late 1964. The other side of the Antechamber is reached in 116.26 inches, or 2082, which then enters another low passage running from 2082 to 2182. The entrance to the King's Chamber represents 2182, while its final wall and ending is reached in 2388. Only time will tell!

of the millennial age and final test for humanity at AD 2914.

Davidson, co-author of *The Great Pyramid: Its Divine Message*, identified the low passage between the Antechamber and the King's Chamber as representing the period 1928 to 1936; in one sense the narrowing of this passage does reflect the conditions of the Depression following the Wall Street crash of 1929.

Max Toth's interpretation of the measurements highlights July 1992 as the end of the passageway and the beginning of what he terms as "end time". Toth predicts fierce storms and volcanic eruptions from 1995. He claims that a Kingdom of the Spirit (after Joachim of Fiore) will emerge after a period of tribulations ending in the collapse of civilization in AD 2025. The Messiah will appear in the sky in AD 2034 and six years later will assume a human appearance and live on Earth for 76 years.

Flinders Petrie dismissed the supposed correlation between human history and the passages of the Great Pyramid by re-surveying the Pyramid and correcting Smyth's errors of mea-

A NEW CHAMBER IN THE GREAT PYRAMID

Hidden passageways point to Sirius

In early 1993 a German researcher, Rudolf Gantenbrink, discovered a new chamber in the Great Pyramid. Using a remote-controlled device, he probed to the end of a 45 degree sloping air duct 210 feet (65 metres) long and only 8 inches (20 centimetres) wide and high. At the end of this passage is a miniature stone

door, possibly made of alabaster or yellow limestone with possibly grooves to slide it upwards. A scatter of fine black dust suggests the presence of organic material and a considerable chamber the other side of sufficient size to allow air currents to circulate.

It is inconceivable that tomb robbers have gained access to the passageway, so the contents of the chamber must be intact. The chamber is situated deep in the rock of the pyramid, some 65 feet (21.5 metres) above the floor of the King's Chamber and 80 feet (25 metres) from the outer facing of the pyramid, on an alignment possibly directly opposite the mysterious Dog Star Sirius, associated with the goddess Isis. Coincidentally (or perhaps not) the distance vertically between the Queen's Chamber and the King's Chamber is also precisely 65 feet (21.5 metres).

The 60-Year Cycle

In 1985 Dr Ravi Batra published a book in which he accurately predicted the onset of the recession in 1989.

The Chinese zodiac, which repeats five times before the Great Cycle has passed

According to Dr Batra, this recession would be characterized by a great increase in unemployment, a decrease in inflation, a rapid fall in property prices and a marked rise in business failures – all adverse economic events which came true in many countries around the world.

Dr Batra suggested that real estate investments should be sold at the end of 1989 and business indebtedness should be reduced – perfect timing, as it turns out. Yet he never claimed to be a prophet, merely a close observer of economic cycles. Dr. Batri has compared events of the 1990s with those of the 1930s. According to his reckoning, 1996 will mark the end of this recession, just as 1936 marked the end of the previous one. The study of cycles might well be a useful adjunct in determining the timing of prophecies.

Sixty years is a recurring timespan to be found in many cultures. It is, for example, the exact time specified by the ancient Chinese for the completion of one "Great Year', during which all possible combinations of events as described by the interaction of the 10 Celestial Stems and 12 Earthly Branches of Chinese metaphysics are supposed to happen. After 60 years, everyone comes back to exactly the same Chinese year combination of Branch and Stem as the year they were born in.

The sexagenary characters representing the Chinese 60-year period are called dragons. Each has one of the five Chinese elements – Wood, Fire, Earth, Metal and Water – ascribed to it with one of the 12 zodiacal animals.

The Egyptians associated the period of 60 years with Osiris, the god of (among other things) cycles, death and resurrection. The "henti" period of his cycle consisted of two periods, each of 60 years' duration.

The ancient Greeks pinpointed the reason for selecting a 60-year cycle. The Neoplatonist Olympiodorus, who lived in Alexandria, wrote:

"... the sphere of Saturn and the sphere of Jupiter are conjoined with each other in their revolutions, sixty years. For if the sphere of Jupiter comes from the same [place in the heavens] to the same in twelve years, but that of Saturn in thirty years, it is evident that when Jupiter has made five, Saturn will have made two revolutions: for twice thirty is sixty, and so likewise is twelve times five; so that their revolutions will be conjoined in sixty years."

Among the Babylonians, the priest Berossus (flourished 260 BC) mentions three extended periods of time, the "sossus" (60 years) and multiples of it, the "neros" of 600 years and the "sarus" of 3600 years, or 60 squared. Two of the last mentioned amount to just over seven millennia, or one week of God, a period used by the Jews to indicate the completion of a full cycle.

Josephus Flavius, who lived in Rome during the first century AD, tells us that ancient time was divided into periods of 600 years. In the manuscript of *Liber Vaticinationem*, 60 is a key period. Later Nostradamus would express the dating of some of his quatrains in terms of the 60-year conjunctions of Jupiter and Saturn.

All the above precedents indicate that, for the purposes of prediction, it may be more revealing to divide up the past and also the future in cyclical periods of 60 years rather than centuries.

THE SAROS CYCLE

Does the ancient Saros cycle affect the hectic trading cycles of modern finance?

One particularly interesting component of the 60-year cycle is the Saros cycle, which was first discovered by the Chaldeans. The cycle is 6585.32 days' long, or 18 years 10.7 days or the equivalent of 19 eclipse years.

The connection between this cycle and the 60-year cycle is made by dividing 60 by 18. If the answer, 3.333, is then multiplied by 60, we get exactly AD 2000, a further pointer to the prophetic and millennial significance of that year.

We have already seen how the 60-year cycle has been used to predict economic events. The Saros cycle would seem to have a similar potential. Coincidentally, one of the most successful financiers and currency speculators of the 1990s is called George Soros. In the autumn of 1992 his speculative activities against sterling caused the British Treasury to use millions of pounds in a futile support operation. On a bleak day for British self-esteem, "Black Wednesday", the pound was withdrawn from the European Monetary System and allowed to "float", effectively downwards to reflect its true value in the market. Thus, through a series of shrewd speculative gambles, Mr Soros added the pound to a list of devaluations of weak European currencies.

It is not known whether Soros relies on business instinct or a proper method of calculation. Some "bets" on currency markets are based on the use of charts revealing cyclical fluctuations. It is possible that the Soros cycle of just over 18 years was involved in George Soros' calculations. Certainly, the movements of the pound in 1974, 18 years earlier, make interesting reading.

Sunspots – The Sun's Cycle

A feature of the surface of the Sun which varies from day to day is its sunspots. These correspond with a clear cycle which matches the rotational cycle of Jupiter.

Sunspots are areas of lower temperature which appear as black spots by contrast with the rest of the Sun's surface. They have been known to man since ancient times, when enormous ones visible to the naked eye were supposed to herald important events. They were first recorded in Europe in 1610, but only in detail from the beginning of the 18th century. Samuel Schwabe was the first to discover their periodic rise and fall, in 1843. In China they have been observed since AD 188.

For the most part, sunspots occur just north or just south of the Sun's equator, between 10 and 30 degrees north or south; they are never seen near the Sun's poles. They have strong magnetic fields which change in polarity according to the cycle. The average spot lasts for a week before it "decays"; some last only a day and some for several months. A large sunspot may cover an area five times the width of the Earth.

For reasons nobody fully understands, sunspot activity seems to follow a pattern, occurring in regular cycles which are virtually identical to the 11.86 year Jupiter cycle. There was an extremely high peak from 1947 to 1950, and an even larger one in 1957. These peaks of activity seem to be accelerating as we reach the end of the millennium. It may be that large numbers of sunspots are indicative of some kind of basic change in the relationship of the Sun to the Earth and the rest of the solar system.

At one time science was baffled by sunspots and offered various explanations: for example, Kirchhoff identified

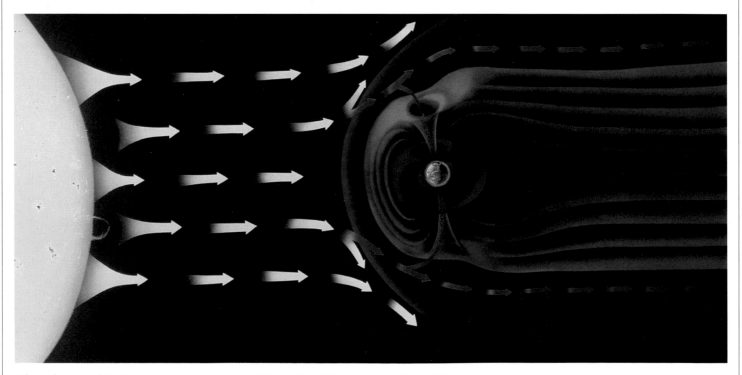

The solar wind (yellow arrows) interacts with the Earth's magnetosphere (blue arrows)

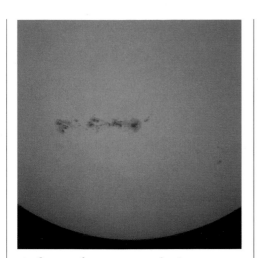

A cluster of sunspots on the Sun

In recent years an enormous amount of computer time and effort has been expended on trying to correlate sunspot activity with a variety of other phenomena, ranging from stock market cycles to tree growth rings. Trees certainly show an 11-year cycle in their rings, but there is as yet little evidence to support the notion of a connection between sunspots and economic cycles.

An interesting correlation from which no satisfactory conclusions have yet been drawn is that between peak sunspot activity and periods of intensive UFO sighting, as well as periods of variation in the Earth's magnetic declination.

them as solar clouds; Zollner, less imaginatively, as slag deposits; and Hale, appropriately perhaps, as electromagnetic storms. There is a definite connection between magnetic storms and large sunspots, and for 60 years or more it has been accepted that climatic changes on the Earth, such as exceptionally high rainfall and severe drought, have been connected with their cycle. Climatic aberrations are becoming more frequent as we approach the millennium and it may be that sunspots will play a part in the cyclical climax arriving around the year AD 2000. The planets are thought to affect sunspot activity, an idea that ties in with the expected changes predicted for May 2000 when the planets will line up against the Earth.

Each outbreak of sunspots is accompanied by an upsurge in the emission of every kind of solar energy, X-rays, ultraviolet, radio waves and visible light. This energy emission, called the solar wind, causes significant changes in the Earth's environment. It may well be that these changes will herald a cataclysmic event at the end of the century.

SUNSPOTS, WEATHER AND THE PLANETS

Do sunspots affect the drought cycle?

Meteorologists recognize the effect of the 11.5-year sunspot cycle on the weather. A great increase in sunspot activity produces a heavily ionized solar wind which causes bad weather on Earth, resulting in poor harvests and higher crop prices. The correlation between a rash of sunspots and storms seems strongest in certain parts of the world, such as Siberia, Scandinavia, the West Indies, southeastern USA and possibly the South Pacific.

The sunspot cycle has also been shown to correlate with shifts in the jetstream. Wild weather is more likely to happen at both solar maxima and minima. The next minima which might well provoke more wild weather is 1999, just before the millennium.

The sunspot cycle has been used successfully to predict drought. In the 1950s it was prophesied that severe drought would occur in 1975/6; in Britain these years turned out to be the hottest and driest summers on record this century. According to the cycle, 1998 and 2021 will also be years of severe drought. The former date fits in with other prophecies of famine and drought leading up to the millennium.

Professor Wood of Colorado University has discovered a mega sunspot cycle of 179 years. Thus in 1778 the number of sunspots was very high, in fact a record. Exactly 179 years later, in 1957, a new peak for sunspot activity was recorded. A report written for NASA by Prescott Sleeper in 1972 suggested that this might have been due to Jupiter, Saturn and Uranus coming into a three-way conjunction, by their estimate every 178.9527 years, representing 6 revolutions of Saturn and 15 revolutions of Jupiter.

The Planetary Conjunctions

The significance of the conjunctions of Jupiter and Saturn has a history extending back to the Babylonians, when the planets were used as the time-keepers of the 60-year cycle.

More recently, a great deal of interest has been shown in the degree to which the movements of these two planets influence the Earth's climate.

The first to start the debate rolling were John Gribbin and Stephen Plagemann in a book called *The Jupiter Effect*, in which they tried to show how the configurations of the planets indirectly affect both climatic and geological events on Earth. The authors, one a NASA scientist and the other a former staff writer for the science journal *Nature*, examined sunspot activity, an increase in which they thought could be related to earthquakes. Sunspot activity was also, they believed, associated with the configuration of the planets in the solar system.

These connections might shed light on some ancient mysteries, and also be relevant to events at the end of the millennium. Their first point was that the movement of all the planets in the solar system can and does affect the Sun.

Of all the planets, the one with the greatest effect on the Sun is Jupiter. This influence is brought to bear by its huge mass, which is 318 times that of the Earth. Saturn, 95 times "heavier" than the Earth, is the second largest planet. Obviously, when both planets line up in the same part of the sky, their gravitational effect is reinforced.

Was Jupiter to blame for the massive destruction wrought by this earthquake in Turkey?

Astrology refers to this as conjunction, so we can safely say that astrological conjunctions, particularly those of the two heaviest planets Jupiter and Saturn, have a gravitational effect upon the Sun.

The work of Professor K. D. Wood of the University of Colorado has shown how gravitational pull can result in surface disturbances such as solar flares and increased sunspot activity. In 1973 he graphed sunspot activity against gravitational variations imposed by the heavier planets. Professor Wood's findings explain why the average sunspot cycle of about 11.5 years varies: the changing pattern of the planets increases or decreases sunspot activity.

So sunspots reflect major changes in the Sun's magnetic field, which affects every planet in the solar system. They can ruffle the usual calm of the ionosphere, a layer of atmosphere 200 miles (322 kilometres) above the surface of the Earth composed of ions and charged particles. It is the ionosphere which, when calm, acts as a reflector of radio waves which can be bounced back to Earth. Little wonder, then, that radio transmissions on Earth suffer interference in times of increased sunspot activity. The latter also signals a time of wild and unsettled weather worldwide.

The changes in the electromagnetic field of the Sun also affect the magma under the Earth's crust or lithosphere, producing additional stresses and strains which can only be released by earthquakes, sometimes volcanic activity, and slippage of one tectonic plate against another. Such events often need only a tiny trigger, for the stresses will

ANCIENT PREDICTIONS OF NATURAL DISASTERS

Noah's Flood, an ancient disaster

One astrologer at the court of Ninevah was aware of the connections between astrological conjunctions and natural disasters. More than 2600 years ago, he wrote: "When Mars approaches Jupiter, there will be great devastation in the land." Ninevah lies in an area that is prone to earthquakes, so the priests and astrologers who kept records of such natural phenomena had a range of data on which to work. To be used for the purposes of making a prediction, however, conjunctions of the planets need to be supported by

other astrological configurations.

The Babylonian priest Berossus writes: "All terrestrial things will be consumed when the planets, which now are traversing their different courses, shall all coincide [come into conjunction] in the sign of Cancer, and so be placed that a straight line could pass directly through all their orbs. But the inundation will take place when the same conjunction of the planets shall occur in Capricorn. In the first is the summer, in the last the winter of the year." [Seneca *Nat. Quaest.* III:29].

Censorinus goes further, stating that these are two separate events; the one in the northern hemisphere summer (when the Sun is in Cancer) will be a conflagration, or Ecpyrosis, while the other in winter (when the Sun is in Capricorn) will be a cataclysm or deluge. The Biblical deluge is seen as one example of this. One "Great Year" after Noah's deluge, Censorinus expected the planets to return to the same conjunction and precipitate another Flood.

have already built up to a point where a small additional stress will cause a major catastrophe, like the San Andreas fault slip in California of 18 April 1906, which, incidentally, occurred shortly after a conjunction of Jupiter and Pluto. Another recent example is the earthquake in Turkey of 22 May 1971, which occurred in the same month as a conjunction of Jupiter

and Neptune. The earthquake in the Liaoning province in Manchuria in February 1975 coincided with a conjunction of Jupiter and Venus.

The conjunction of Jupiter and Saturn causes not just sunspots but the type of events which the ancient prophets always associated with the apocalypse: turbulent weather, earthquakes and volcanic activity.

Christ's
SECRETS

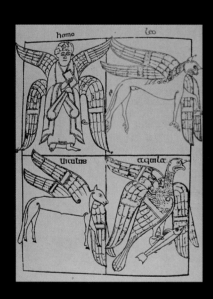

Some of the teachings imparted by Christ to his disciples remain secrets to all but a few to this day. Hostages to scholarship, and long lost to the Church, the manuscripts which contain these secrets may shed much needed light on what awaits us at the millennium.

Early Christian Prophecies

In the New Testament, both John the Baptist and Jesus are called prophets, men who continue the tradition of conveying the will of God to His people.

Jesus was sometimes taken to be a reincarnation of one of the ancient prophets. In Mark 8:27, he asks "Whom do men say that I am?" The consensus of opinion seems to have been that he was a reincarnation of either John the Baptist, Elias, or one of the Old Testament prophets. It is hard to see how he could have been a reincarnation of the prophet by whom he was baptized, but that has not deterred the believers in this theory.

In the next chapter of Mark (9:1), Jesus makes a prophecy about the

Many thought Jesus was just a prophet

coming kingdom of God: "Verily I say unto you, that there be some of them that stand here, which shall not taste of death, till they have seen the kingdom of God come with power."

It is no wonder that many early Christians expected the end of the world and the coming of the kingdom of God within their lifetime. They would have been even more surprised to learn that after two millenniums it has still not arrived. Jesus may have been speaking in the personal sense of initiation into the mysteries of the kingdom of God before their death, but many must have read his words as a prediction of the end of the world.

This prospect of the arrival of the kingdom of God arose again after 1000 years, and again in the year 1033, one millennium after the death of Christ. Another favourite millennial year was 1666, 1000 years after the birth of Christ plus 666, the number of the Second Beast of the Apocalypse of St John. Now, the imminent arrival of the end of the second millennium is supported by astrological and indeed astronomically significant signs and

"heavenly markers" which have led many observers to wonder if perhaps ours really is the time predicted so many generations ago.

In the time of the early Christian church, members who had the special gift of uttering words (sometimes in foreign languages) while in a trance were called prophets, thus expanding the pre-Christian idea of specially trained and "contacted" prophets. These people, sometimes also called "charismatics", were "inspired" by God with an intelligible message. They were very different from so-called "speakers in tongues", who babbled in a language that unintelligible to their listeners.

After the death of its founder Christianity fought a long, hard struggle against the pagan cults. Many strange doctrines derived from the Greeks, many of whom were early literate converts to Christianity. It is not often realized that all the New Testament scriptures were written in Greek – a language that Jesus himself did not speak.

Much of the early, more direct, experience of religion, such as "travelling in the spirit" or visiting the third heaven while still alive, have been filtered out of official Christian doctrine. Other Gnostic ideas were squeezed out of mainstream Christian thought to resurface in 20th-century theosophy or occultism.

The wonderfully detailed images of the Apocalypse of St John have been drawn on ever since they were written, by people attempting to pierce the veil of the future and determine what the turn of the millennium may have in store for us.

Christ was sometimes thought to be a reincarnation of John the Baptist

WHAT IS ESCHATOLOGY?

Eschatology, a Greek word meaning "last discourse", is the doctrine of the four last things. It is concerned with the events destined to happen at the end of the world, according to Christian doctrines. There are two different aspects to eschatology.

Individual eschatology is concerned with what happens to man after death. Most people regard death as the end of their personal world. Some sects believe that man lies in the grave until the universal judgement at the end of the world. The Seventh-Day Adventists, for example, believe that "the condition of man in death is one of unconsciousness. That all men, good and evil alike, remain in the grave from death to the resurrection" (*Fundamental Beliefs*, article 10).

General eschatology is concerned with what happens to the world at the end of time, which is the subject of the Apocalypses. The four "last things" supposed to happen at that time are:

• The return of Christ, or the Second Coming

• The resurrection of the dead from their graves

• The Last Judgement of the dead and those who are still living at that time (the "quick")

• The final recompense, or separation, into the saved and the damned.

Resurrection and Vampires

The early Christians believed in bodily resurrection. Their conviction was that human life is inseparable from bodily experience: if a man comes back to life from the dead, he must come back in physical form.

Bloodthirsty Dracula, later a vampire

The Resurrection of Christ

The early Christian fathers Irenaeus and Tertullian both emphasized the anticipation of bodily resurrection. The Gnostic Christians on the other hand, who ridiculed the concept of bodily resurrection, thought that spiritual resurrection was the norm and frequently devalued the body, considering its actions unimportant to the "spiritual body".

Christ's resurrection is a central tenet of Christianity. If he had not risen from the dead, he would be considered as just another spiritual teacher. Some religions celebrate cycles of life, death and rebirth in other forms, and only Christianity insists on the return to life of one individual, Jesus Christ. This new departure in religious thought represented a turning point in world history. Despite the specific statement in the Christian scriptures that Jesus of Nazareth was "crucified, dead, and buried" and rose "on the third day", many modern theologians seem to be uncomfortable with the idea of his physical resurrection. Christ, so the scriptures tell us, ate a piece of fish to demonstrate to his disciples that he was not a ghost, and even asked Thomas to feel the wound in his side.

Tertullian (c. AD 190) defined the orthodox viewpoint by stating that "as Christ rose bodily from the grave, so every believer should anticipate the resurrection of the flesh . . .The salvation of the soul I believe needs no discussion . . . What is raised is this flesh, suffused with blood, built up with bones, interwoven with nerves, entwined with veins". Tertullian goes on to declare that anyone who denies the resurrection of the flesh is a heretic, which presumably means that many modern Christians are heretics.

The phrase "suffused with blood" has a familiar ring, for it has been used in almost every description of a vampire ever penned! A vampire is one who has risen from his grave some time before the general resurrection of the dead, and who troubles his neighbours by slaking his thirst for blood at their expense. If you believe, as did the early Christians, in a bodily resurrection, then a vampire is simply un-dead before his time.

There are many strange parallels between orthodox Christian belief and belief in vampires. The early Christians, for example, specifically used catacombs, underground charnel houses, as places of worship (see panel). From time immemorial, particularly in eastern Europe, there has been a tradition of vampire resurrections from such tombs. Those who have become vampires have become so by having had their blood drunk by an existing vampire. Interestingly, the central sacrament of Christianity has been the drinking of the blood of Christ. This was first done on the night before his death and became, as a consequence, a part of Christian practice.

The communion consumption of Christ's blood is accompanied by a rubric suggesting that this blood offers life everlasting. Tradition has it that vampires also live forever, or at least for very long periods of time. The cure for vampires is said to be a stake in the heart. Eccarius pointed out that the centurion's lance thrust into the side of Christ was designed to save any further pain by killing the man on the cross, and should effectively have prevented a resurrection.

The story of St Peter denying his Lord three times before cock-crow receives an echo in vampire folklore, which holds that the vampire must return to his tomb before cock-crow.

As if to prove the generality of physical resurrection, in St Matthew it is recorded (27:50–53) that at the time of Christ's death upon the cross a number of other men who were dead rose from their graves and roamed the streets: "the earth did quake, and the rocks rent; and the graves were opened; and many bodies . . . came out of the graves after his resurrection, and went into the holy city [Jerusalem], and appeared unto many."

The spine-chilling film vampire Nosferatu

CATACOMBS AND CHRISTIANS

Why were many early Christian ceremonies held in catacombs, the old Roman underground necropolises? This cannot have been entirely because of fear of persecution, as is often suggested. On the contrary, worshippers could easily have been trapped in such places by Roman soldiers. Nor is there any evidence to suggest that early Christians lived in the catacombs to facilitate worship. Even in those repressive times, believers managed to meet in houses.

The most plausible reason for using the catacombs for services is intimately connected with the belief in resurrection at the time of the Second Coming. In the minds of the early Christians there was a very close link between the life and death of their founder, Christ, and the bodies of their own dead, whom they confidently expected to undergo physical resurrection on the Day of Judgement, a day they expected at any time. It was appropriate, therefore, for the whole community of the "quick" and the dead to worship in the same place. Until fairly recently the illustrious dead were still buried inside churches, further evidence of the close relationship between the dead and the living in Christian thought.

The Apocalypse of St John

The Apocalypse of St John the Divine lies at the heart of this book, because it contains prophecies of what will happen if AD 2000 is indeed the year of the Apocalypse.

The Apocalypse of St John, written in AD 96 (see panel), refers back to the Old Testament books of the prophets no less than 285 times, and is in substance a continuation of the apocalyptic works of Daniel and Ezekiel. Like Ezekiel, St John eats of a strange and obviously psychedelic little book (10:10) which enables him to see what the future holds. Interestingly, the writer George Bernard Shaw once flippantly dismissed the Apocalypse as the product of a drug addict's fevered imagination!

The Apocalypse of St John is highly structured and numerological in its approach. It has 22 chapters, like the 22 letters of the Hebrew alphabet, and groups many of its symbols and scenes into sevens. The 7th, 10th, half the 11th, and 14th chapters are written as asides from the main narrative and could be removed without much loss of coherency. The opening three chapters of the Apocalypse consist of St John's letters and warnings to the seven branches of the fledgling Christian Church in Asia Minor (modern Turkey).

During his vision St John has a conversation with the Spirit, described as "the first and the last . . . in his right hand seven stars: and out of his mouth went a sharp two-edged sword" (1:16). This Spirit, identified as the "Word of God" (19:13), variously threatens to

St John the Divine's vision of the crowned Lamb surrounded by harp players

"fight against them [the churches] with the sword in my mouth" (2:16) or "rule them with a rod of iron" (2:27) or blot out the name of their members from the book of life. Later in the book (19:11–15) he is shown as a crowned warrior on a white horse. None of the descriptions of this being remotely resemble the Christ figure as he is usually depicted.

The truly apocalyptic part of the book begins with the opening of a door in heaven (chapter 3) through which St John enters "in the spirit", just like the entry of St Paul into the third heaven. As he loses consciousness and leaves his body, the voice calling the prophet sounds distant and brassy, like a trumpet. St John immediately sees a figure seated upon a throne. The figure, which most commentators have taken to be Christ, looks as if it is made of "jasper and a sardine stone" (a sard or sardonyx), and is surrounded by a rainbow. Seven spirits of God are seated in front of the throne and around it are grouped 24 crowned elders. As in Ezekiel's vision of the flying throne of Jehovah, the throne flashes with lightning.

Also in evidence in St John's vision are the same four beasts, or cherubim, that Ezekiel saw around Jehovah, resembling a lion, a calf, a man, and an eagle, but all with six wings and studded with many eyes. "Thousands of thousands" of angels surround these strange beings. The Christ figure holds a mysterious book in one hand. A lamb which has been slain, symbolic of Christ, offers to open this book which no man is able to open. The lamb, which has seven horns and seven eyes, is related to one of the many-horned beasts that are encountered later in the Apocalypse.

The lamb opens the seven seals of the book, one by one. A portion of God's wrath is released upon humanity with the opening of each seal. Then John hears the seven trumpets, signalling the release of further horrors, namely several beasts and prophets. Next, seven vials are poured over long-suffering mankind.

Finally, the "Word of God" returns riding a white horse and wearing many crowns, in his mouth a sharp sword and accompanied by a company of heavenly troops. With these troops he vanquishes the Beast and the kings of the Earth. As John said, "the time is at hand" – words that are equally relevant at the present time, as we rapidly approach the Apocalypse that is expected at the end of the 20th century.

THE MYSTERY OF REVELATION

"Revelation", sometimes referred to as the Apocalypse of St John, contains one of the most extraordinary visions ever recorded. Through this vision St John was shown what will happen at the end of the world, at the time of the resurrection and judgement of the dead, and was given a premonition of the 1000 years of peaceful rule thereafter.

The authorship of "Revelation" is disputed, with some claiming that an individual called Cerinthus "borrowed" the name of St John the Apostle to add weight to his own writings. The one certainty that is connected with the work is the date it came into being, about AD 96.

"Revelation" is so rich in imagery that it could almost be a manual for one of the pagan initiatory religions of the period rather than a book of the New Testament.

Various legends have grown up around "Revelation". One is that St John experienced his vision on the Greek volcanic island of Patmos. In

Ephesus, burial place of St John

later life, St John is said to have chosen to be entombed at Ephesus, the final resting place of the Virgin Mary. After selecting his vault the Apostle allegedly closed the entrance upon himself and was never seen again. It was believed that he would sleep in this tomb until the Second Coming of Christ, when he would rise from the dead, presumably to confirm the truth of his vision. The Second Coming of Christ, therefore, is very likely to be accompanied by the second coming of St John.

Unholy Beasts

Through the ages, various human bogeymen have been associated with the terrible Antichrist. In the time of the Romans, it was the emperors themselves who were linked with him, and latterly churchmen and politicians.

Was the eagle-headed god of Assyria the origin of one of the Apocalyptic beasts?

Protestant antipathy for the Roman Catholic Church led to the Pope being identified as the Antichrist. In the 19th century, Napoleon was identified as the Antichrist and in the 20th century Hitler was Nostradamus's candidate for the second Antichrist. Strangely, the Antichrist is not even mentioned by name in the Apocalypse. The Greek word *antichristos* only occurs in the first and second gospels of St John.

The Beast is another perplexing figure in the Apocalypse. He has been identified with many historical figures, right down to Aleister Crowley in the present century. A number of beasts crop up in the Apocalypse and are often confused with each other. Two separate Greek words are used for the Beast, *zoon* and *therion*.

Zoon, or living creatures, is used for the four holy beasts, which have the heads of the lion, calf, man and the eagle. Similar to the cherubim of Ezekiel, they have six wings embedded with many eyes. They are the four beasts found on the last tarot card, and their job is to guard the throne of Jehovah or the entrance to the lower heavens. They may also be derived from the Assyrian astral gods Marduk (the winged bull), Nebo (with human features), Nergal (a winged lion) and Ninib (an eagle).

The Greek word *therion*, however, is used to describe altogether wilder beasts. The first of these is the "beast that ascendeth out of the bottomless pit" (11:7). This beast may possibly be the same as the first Beast, which will "rise up out of the sea, having seven heads and ten horns, and upon those horns ten crowns, and upon its heads the name of blasphemy . . . like unto a leopard" (13:1-8). To this polymorphic beast, which has the feet of a bear and the mouth of a lion, "the dragon gave him his power, and his seat, and great authority".

In Daniel chapter 7, it is suggested that the three great Gentile empires are referred to here: the lion of Babylon, the bear of Persia and the leopard of Greece. Nowadays, the bear is of course equated with Russia. The ten horns are often equated with the Roman Empire, the horns being ten kings (Daniel 7:24).

Many commentators have suggested that the rise of a new pan-European power, the European Union, is a further sign of the immediacy of the apocalypse. Before this prophecy comes true, it is claimed, membership of the Union will rise in number to 13 states and then decline to 10. The theory has been put forward that the first Beast might even be a dictatorial leader of the EU (see panel).

The first Beast will be put on his throne by the Dragon, usually identified as Satan. He will reign for 42 years. If the first Beast's reign starts in 1995, as has been suggested by some, then it will last until 2037. During this period, both the Dragon and the Beast will be worshipped.

The second Beast has "two horns like a lamb, and he spake as a dragon . . . he maketh fire come down from heaven on the earth . . . and his number is 666" (13:11–18). This Beast is the most infamous of all. His speaking as a dragon allies him with Satan. He inherits the power of the first Beast and performs miracles, including bringing fire from heaven, like Prometheus, in full view of witnesses.

This second Beast is the antithesis of the lamb that symbolizes Christ, and is often identified as being the Antichrist. The second Beast causes a statue to be put up for the worship of the first Beast, and enables the statue to speak, just as Simon Magus caused statues to speak and appear to live. The second Beast is mentioned again with the false prophet in Daniel 19:19–20, 20:4 and 20:10.

St John the Divine identifies this second Beast by the number 666. Many have taken this to mean that John was writing about Nero, a nebulous connection to say the very least. More significantly, St John prophesies that when the second Beast comes to power no one will be allowed to buy or sell without wearing his mark on either their right hand or on their forehead.

The second Beast will be finally overcome by the warrior on a white horse called "The Word of God" and be cast into a lake of fire and brimstone together with his false prophet. His supporters will be eaten by carrion birds specially called by an angel for this purpose.

THE SCARLET WHORE AND THE EURO-BEAST

The scarlet Whore riding on the Beast

The first Beast is probably the same as that called "a scarlet coloured beast, full of names of blasphemy, having seven heads and ten horns" (17:3) and carrying the Whore on its back. The Whore was "arrayed in purple and scarlet colour, and decked with gold and precious stones and pearls, having a golden cup in her hand full of abominations and filthiness of her fornication", and on her head was a label proclaiming her "Mystery, Babylon the Great, the mother of harlots and abominations of the earth" (17:5). The Whore also drinks the blood of saints and martyrs, which her mount the Beast aims to destroy.

The seven heads of the first Beast are explained in 17:10 as seven kings, of whom "five are fallen, and one is, and the other is not yet come". The ten horns are interpreted as "ten kings, which have received no kingdom as yet". These ten horns or kings "shall hate the whore, and shall make her desolate and naked, and shall eat her flesh, and burn her with fire" (17:16). They treat the Beast somewhat better, giving their ten kingdoms to him. This passage has been interpreted as the surrendering of the sovereignty of 12 European countries to a central European parliament.

The Last Judgement

The idea of the judgement of the soul after death is ancient, dating from before 2400 BC, and widespread.

The Last Judgement

Satan, leader of the rebel angels

The ancient Egyptians believed that the soul implored the heart not to give evidence against it at the time of judgement. Judaism did not originally include immediate personal judgement, which was conceived more as a trial of nations at the end of time. The 1st-century AD Nag Hammadi Gnostic Christian codexes suggest that the body can give evidence against the soul in the judgement process. The penalty for misdeeds was rejection from heaven and reincarnation in a new body.

Neoplatonism introduced the idea of initiation into a "Mystery" cult giving real benefits in the afterlife by admitting the initiate to heavens he might not otherwise reach. This represented a departure from Homeric thinking, which did not allow for life after death.

The early Christians assumed that Christ would return for the second time within their lifetime, usher them into a perfect world and administer punishments to their persecutors.

When it became obvious that Christ might not return for 1000 years, a different idea was adopted, of the dead undergoing a preliminary judgement just after their death but then waiting in the grave, or perhaps in purgatory, for a final appraisal. At this so-called Last Judgement the dead will be resurrected to undergo examination of their moral worth. This judgement, however, will not happen until the events outlined in the earlier chapters of the Apocalypse of St John have taken place. Christ has to come again to take up the job of the awful judge, whereupon the dead will be summoned to his presence by the sound of the final trumpet blast.

In medieval England the Last Judgement came to be known as the Doom, when it was considered that individuals could expect either heavenly bliss or torment in the lake of fire. After this, time will cease and history give way to eternity in which there is no more death, sorrow or pain. Paintings of this period often depicted the scene as the Archangel Michael weighing the souls of the dead. Similarly, the ancient Egyptians showed the weighing of the heart against the feather of truth.

The pattern of judgement and resurrection had become quite complicated by the time St John put pen to paper. According to his writings, the first judgement will take place when Christ comes among mankind a second time. The souls of martyrs who have not worshipped the second Beast will be immediately reprieved and live in paradise with Christ during his 1000 years of rule. This is called the first resurrection.

The early martyrs certainly deserved God's favour, if the many gory paintings depicting their martyrdom are accurate. The dead who could not match their magnificent example of faith will be left in their graves until the end of Christ's 1000-year rule. At the end of this period, Satan, or the Dragon, will again be on the loose and making trouble by deceiving the living. Then the second and final judgement will take place. On this occasion, judgement will be made on the basis of what has been written of the dead man's deeds in the Book of Life. Woe betide anyone without an entry in this book, for he or she will be cast forever into the lake of fire, along with Death himself. Such a sentence is called "the second death".

ADVANCE RESERVATIONS IN HEAVEN

Those chosen to be saved from damnation will be pre-marked and belong to one of the tribes of Israel, according to chapter 7 of the Apocalypse. The passage dealing with this aspect of the Last Judgement has encouraged many Christian sects to believe that only 144,000 will be saved. In the Apocalypse an angel "seals" the foreheads of 12,000 members of each of the tribes of Israel with "the seal of the living God", hence the total of 144,000.

This seal is very similar to the mark imposed by the Beast upon his followers, and in both cases serves to show which "side" the individual is on. It is also the origin of Joanna Southcott's seal with which she made up "heavenly passes" for her followers. As ten of the tribes of Israel are currently "lost" or dispersed, it is easy to see how the concern to reunite them grew into a major millennial concern for 18th-century Christians.

The benefit of being sealed could be said to be the same as that of having secured an advanced booking for heaven.

Could the Last Judgement be finally close at hand?

False Second Comings

In the second century AD one group of Christians believed that the heavenly version of the city of Jerusalem was going to materialize in the clouds and descend to Earth.

Jim Jones, false Messiah

The group called the Montanists was founded in Phrygia around AD 156. Their leader, the prophet Montanus, practised ecstatic prophecy together with his priestesses, Prisca and Maximilla, who preached that the end of the world was at hand.

Asceticism and voluntary martyrdom were also part of the creed of Montanus. In fact, the sect was a throwback to the apocalyptic beliefs and desires of early Christianity which had almost been eradicated from the teachings of the orthodox church by this time. The best-known member of the Montanists was perhaps Tertullian.

Believing that Christ would reappear in the town of Pepuza in Syria, the followers of Montanus established a large community there to await him. Accusations of a number of vices were levelled at Montanist prophets, who were accused of dying their hair, painting their eyelids, gambling and staging sacred dances with virgins. The Montanists particularly venerated the rich imagery of the Apocalypse of St John and claimed to have the apostle's tomb, a distinction

that was also claimed by the pagan city of Ephesus.

In AD 550 the Bishop of Ephesus dug up the corpses of Montanus and his prophetesses and ritually burnt them, thereby hoping to stamp out this troublesome cult. Despite its best efforts, however, orthodox Christianity did not finally succeed in this aim until the 6th century AD.

The Montanists were not the only sect to claim knowledge of the second

coming of Christ. Some sects have mixed the claim with promises of resurrection and eternal life and in so doing have encouraged mass suicide. One example of this is provided by the 900 members of the so-called People's Temple in Jonestown, Guyana, whose leader, Jim Jones, persuaded them to follow him to the grave.

Another, equally disturbing case occurred in the Ukrainian capital, Kiev, in November 1993, when

Maria Devi Christos, modern Russian Messiah

33-year-old Marina Tsvyguna, the leader of a sect called the Great White Brotherhood, declared herself to be the Messiah, Maria Devi Christos. Her mission, she claimed, was to save mankind from the approaching millennial doom. Like other prophets before her, Maria had claimed that only 144,000 of her elect would be saved.

In her role as the returned Christ, Maria dressed in white, wore a strange peaked hat, a shepherd's crook like that of the ancient Egyptian pharaohs, a crucifix and bead jewellery. Together with her second husband, Krivonogov, a former youth leader who had received training in psychological warfare, she expressed the wish that her followers would follow her to the grave and beyond. The couple used a combination of old-style religious exhortation and the latest brainwashing techniques to achieve their goal. Thousands of well-educated children from good homes who had joined the cult were persuaded to break all contact with their families and to slowly starve themselves to ensure their resurrection with Maria in heaven. Like other prophets before her, Maria claimed that only 144,000 of her elect would be saved. Post-hypnotic suggestions kept the children's attention fixed on a distant realm of light, reached only via the grave. Fortunately, the Ukrainian authorities intervened and jailed the "messiah" before any of her victims died.

The Russians have a long history of mass religious suicide in the expectation of better times to come. Maria's Great White Brotherhood had a ready-made precedent in the obscure Russian religious sect called the "Old Believers". During the late 17th and early 18th century at least 20,000 of them burned themselves to death rather than accept state religious orthodoxy. One extremist Russian Christian sect, called the Krasnye Krestinnye or Fire Baptists, would commit mass suicide by assembling with their family and friends in a house which they would then systematically set on fire, like the holocaust at the end of the Waco siege in April 1993. In one such Russian mass suicide, in the Paleostrovski monastery, over 2700 men, women and children burned themselves to death.

THE FIRST COMING OF CHRIST

St John also relates the secret history of the first coming of Christ, which was obviously part of the more extended war between God who wishes to incarnate his Son in a sinful world, and Satan (in the form of a Dragon) who wishes to avoid this at all costs.

The spiritual side of the action is played out in heaven. The Dragon (in Greek, *drakon*) and the Woman both appear as "a great wonder in heaven", and represent Satan and the Virgin Mary. The Dragon may also have astrological connections, for the dragon's tail covers a "third part of the stars of heaven" (12:4). The Dragon is introduced as the persecutor of the woman who is "clothed with the sun, and [has] the moon under her feet, and upon her head [wears] a crown of twelve stars" (12:1). She is pregnant and is suffering the pangs of childbirth. The Dragon, which is red in colour and has seven crowned heads and ten horns, waits for the child to be delivered so it can kill and eat him. God, however, intervenes and saves the child from the dragon's jaws, so that he may carry out his appointed role as saviour.

The Apocalypse then says that the woman flees into the wilderness, where God feeds her for 1260 days. The Dragon persecutes her, even causing floods in an attempt to engulf her. On the assumption that the woman is Mary, mother of Christ, and using the "year for a day" rule, the period of her stay in the wilderness is 1260 years after the birth of Christ. In an earlier verse (11:3), power is granted to two witnesses to prophesy for 1260 days before they are killed by the beast from the bottomless pit (11:7). These two witnesses are later resurrected, echoing Christ's resurrection.

Satan, Sin and Death

The Seven Seals, Seven Trumpets

The Lamb, symbol of Christ, is due to open the seals of the secret book of the Apocalypse of St John at the end of the millennium and release all kinds of horrors onto the Earth.

The Lamb, symbol of Christ in the Apocalypse

The first four seals of the secret book of the Apocalypse of St John will release the legendary Four Horsemen of the Apocalypse (6:1–8) who will torment mankind (see panel).

The fifth seal will reveal something quite different – the souls of martyrs found underneath an altar, crying out for revenge against their murderers (6:9–11). The next two seals are purely concerned with natural disasters and ecological doom. The Apocalypse describes earthquakes, the removal of the ozone layer ("the heaven was removed as a scroll when it is rolled up"), meteorites ("the stars of heaven fell upon the earth") and many other natural disasters.

The opening of the seventh seal will initiate the next sequence of seven, the blowing of the seven trumpets by angels. These seven trumpet blasts will bring down disaster on the heads of those not favoured with God's seal. One angel will hurl the contents of a lighted incense burner onto Earth, causing thunder, lightning and earthquakes. These terrible disasters will destroy one-third of all sea creatures and one-third of all shipping.

One event of particular interest is the fall of a meteorite called "Wormwood", which will poison all the rivers and many people; it is also possible that "Wormwood" will turn out to be a man-made bomb. The fall of this meteorite, heralded by the fifth trumpet blast, will open the "bottomless pit" and release the armies of the angel Abaddon (in Greek Apollyon) to destroy mankind. His hideous soldiers are like locusts but with human faces and crowns. They are winged with powerful scorpion-like stings in their

Angelic trumpeters of the Apocalypse

tails which produce lingering illness in victims. These were the creatures that Charles Manson and his "family" hoped to unleash on an undeserving world through a spate of killings.

The sixth trumpet will release four angels previously "bound in the Euphrates river". From this description they sound more like spirits, or jinn, who were often put in lead bottles by magicians and thrown into a river or the sea; King Solomon is reputed to have done this to the recalcitrant spirits he used to build his Temple. These four will be accompanied by 200,000,000 horsemen whose job it is to kill a third of what remains of mankind – for angels, they seem a remarkably bloodthirsty bunch.

The seventh and last trumpet blast will occur when the "kingdoms of this world are become the kingdoms of our Lord, and of his Christ". It will herald the resurrection of the dead and their judgement by God.

One final series of horrors is still to come, though. The seven angels, clothed in pure white linen with golden girdles, will appear bearing seven golden vials. Each of these vials contains a plague to be inflicted on mankind. The contents of the first vial will give sores to those with the Beast's mark; the second will kill every form

of life in and on the seas; the third will turn the rivers to blood, further poisoning the water supplies; the fourth, taking its power from the sun, will scorch mankind; the fifth vial will darken the kingdom of the Beast; the sixth will dry up the Euphrates River to allow the kings of the East to invade Israel and perhaps Europe, as is also foretold by Nostradamus. The final vial will poison the atmosphere with previously unknown infections.

Thus the seven seals are opened, the seven trumpets blast out their individual messages of destruction and the seven vials are poured upon mankind. Only those protected with "the seal of God" will be spared these tribulations.

THE FOUR HORSEMEN OF THE APOCALYPSE

The fourth Horsemen of the Apocalypse, Death, issuing from the jaws of Hell

The first horseman rides on a white horse, carries a bow, and wears a crown: he is usually called Conquest. The second rides on a blood-red horse, wields a great sword and is sometimes depicted dressed in black armour: he is usually called War. Wars have always been associated with the end of the world.

The third horseman rides a black horse and holds a balance in his hand. Sometimes he is depicted as a monk. He symbolizes Famine; in the vision of St John this association is emphasized by a voice quoting the prices of wheat and barley, staple foods which were eight times what they should have been. The prophecy is that there will be severe shortages of these staples in the final days, as predicted by Nostradamus.

The fourth horseman, who rides a light-coloured horse, is Death. He is usually depicted as a skeleton, and is sometimes also called Plague or Pestilence. Behind him comes Hell, sometimes shown as the jaws of a disembodied head belching flames.

St Mark's Apocalypse

Chapter 13 of St Mark's Gospel is a mini-Apocalypse every bit as threatening as the Apocalypse of St John.

On the Mount of Olives Jesus explains to Peter, James, John and Andrew the conditions of his second coming, and the end of the world. The prophecy falls into three distinct phases.

First, Jesus warns of social and political changes to come on Earth. He predicts that there will be many false messiahs, who should be avoided. Before the millennium there will be many wars and rumours of wars, "nation shall rise against nation, and kingdom against kingdom", a prediction dated by Nostradamus for 1999. There will be an increase in earthquakes, famines and related troubles.

Then comes a passage that has puzzled many interpreters: there will be "the abomination of desolation, spoken of by Daniel the prophet, standing where it ought not" (St Mark 13:14). This is said to refer to the introduction by Antiochus Epiphanes (reigned 175–164 BC) of the statue of Zeus into the holy of holies, the Temple of Jerusalem, in an attempt to Hellenize the Jews. This passage is underscored by the parenthetical remark "let him that readeth understand", a very broad hint that the meaning is to be interpreted by one of the secret keys of the Qabalah.

The reference to the Old Testament prophet Daniel is also of interest, for it was he who provided numerical clues as to the arrival of the Apocalypse. Sects like the Jehovah's Witnesses and the Seventh-Day Adventists use the dating from Daniel.

Jesus then advises his followers to flee to the mountains, advice taken by the Essenes, who left Jerusalem for Qumran before the time of this Gospel; the Millerites, who waited in 1843 on the hills for the Second Coming; the Mormons; Aetherius Society members, who made many such pilgrimages, and other groups anticipating the end of the world.

The period of great tribulations involving false prophets and messiahs will be followed by hardships of a different kind, when "the sun shall be darkened, and the moon shall not give her light" (13:24). From Jesus's description these cosmic happenings sound very much like the opening of the sixth seal of the Apocalypse of St John, or the interpretation that Immanuel Velikovsky put on the cosmic events of 1502 BC and 1450 BC, when a huge heavenly body came so close to Earth that it caused the revolution of the globe to falter. It looks as if this event is set to be repeated in the not too distant future: "And the stars

Christ praying in the Garden before vouchsafing the secrets of the end of the world

St Mark, author of the mini-Apocalypse

Christ and his angels will gather the "elect" from the four winds, presumably meaning from the four corners of the Earth. This passage has concentrated the thinking of those prophets who like to think that the "elect" will be drawn exclusively from their particular sects. In the Apocalypse it is suggested that the elect will number only 144,000. The passage concludes with an injunction to be watchful, in case the Second Coming of Christ occurs suddenly and catches the faithful off guard.

Finally, a most perplexing verse occurs in which Jesus says "Verily I say unto you, that this generation shall not pass, till all these things be done" (13:30). Does this mean that Christ's prophecy has failed, because certainly these events have not occurred in the sequence promised? Alternatively, perhaps the word "generation" is intended to refer to the seed and descendants of those who were with him on that day.

These prophecies made a deep impact upon the early Christians. They were repeated almost word for word in Matthew chapters 24–25 and also in Luke 21, and formed an important part of early belief.

JOEL PREDICTS WAR

The Old Testament prophet Joel also had visions of the end of the world, which he called the "day of the Lord". In Joel 2:30–32 he writes of the initial heavenly signs heralding the end of time: "And I will shew wonders in the heavens and in the earth, blood, and fire, and pillars of smoke. The sun shall be turned into darkness, and the moon into blood, before the great and the terrible day of the Lord come." In 3:15 he continues, "the sun and the moon shall be darkened, and the stars shall withdraw their shining."

These events mirror the descriptions of the end of time given elsewhere, except that Joel strikes a more optimistic note than many other prophets of these events: "whosoever shall call on the name of the Lord shall be delivered". Salvation, it seems, can be achieved quite simply, without great sacrifice.

On the down side, however, Joel is less generous to non-believers, threatening to sell the children of the gentile or heathen nations into slavery, and positively warlike. At the time of God's judgement, he plans to "gather all nations and . . . bring them down into the valley of Jehoshaphat" (3:2). Then he calls on the people to prepare for war (3:9), "wake up the mighty men, let all the men of war draw near; let them come up: Beat your plowshares into swords, and your pruning hooks into spears."

The sun is turned into darkness

of heaven shall fall", indicating perhaps a bombardment of the Earth by comets or meteorites.

These cosmic events will be followed by phenomena of a supernatural nature, and Christ himself will be seen "coming in the clouds with great power and glory". This century there have already been several well-documented appearances by the Virgin Mary, with strange effects marking her coming, like the sun moving in the sky in an unnatural way.

SECRETS
of the
GNOSTICS

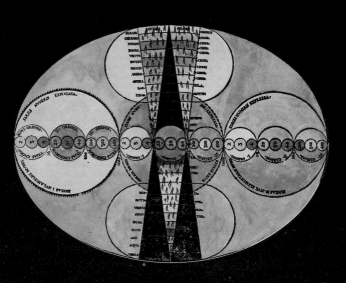

*If the garden of forking paths that is
history had followed the Gnostics,
Christianity might have depended upon
knowledge and individual effort rather
than faith and the intercession of the
Church. Some of the mysteries of
Gnosticism are very relevant to us now
at the end of the millennium.*

The Gnostic Apocalypse

The early Christians were regarded by some as a new Jewish sect who believed they had finally found the long-awaited Messiah and not a new religion.

Clement of Alexandria

The initial Jewish disciples were joined by many Greek converts, who brought their philosophical heritage to the new religion of Christianity. The New Testament was in fact written in Greek, and the Old Testament used by the early Christians was the most ancient Greek translation, known as the Septuagint and made in Alexandria about 255 BC. Christianity may be seen as a Hellenized Jewish sect.

Centres of Greek-speaking Jews, such as at Alexandria, drew their religious inspiration from Hellenistic, Judaic and Egyptian sources. Gnosticism (literally

Symbols speak louder than words

meaning "knowledge") was intertwined with early Christianity, while emphasizing spiritual knowledge rather than merely faith as the road to salvation. Many Gnostics regarded themselves as Christian.

Philo of Alexandria (c. 20 BC–AD 50) was a typical Gnostic. A member of a distinguished family of that city, he was learned both in Jewish knowledge and in the ancient Greek philosophers such as Plato. He originated the doctrine of the "Logos", which was used by St John in his Gospel: "In the beginning was the Word ['Logos' in the original Greek], and the Word [Logos] was with God, and the Word was God."

Thus a basic Christian doctrine was derived from Gnosticism. Many of Philo's ideas appear in the Gospels, notably in the fourth Gospel and in the Pauline Epistle to the Hebrews.

Clement of Alexandria, an early Christian father, said "the Gnosis itself is that which has descended by transmission to a few, having been imparted unwritten by the Apostles" (*Miscell.* Book VI, chapter 7).

Many early Christians were Gnostics, including some of the Apostles. Christianity could well have grown up as a Gnostic religion, emphasizing knowledge above blind acceptance. So what happened?

As in any religion or movement, the successors of the founder decided which things to keep and which to throw out. They discarded the spiritual knowledge of Gnosticism as being too dangerous, and kept the concept of blind acceptance of Church doctrine. Then they declared Gnosticism a heresy. If this had not happened then maybe the Dark Ages would not have been quite so dark, and the classical texts that were destroyed by the thousand would have survived, to leaven civilization. The intolerance of the early church fathers decided to cover up the Gnostic origins of Christianity, plunging Europe into the Dark Ages.

Meanwhile, the classical texts of Greek philosophy and civilization either mouldered away or were partially saved in Arabic translations. With them Islam spread across the Middle East and Northern Africa.

Eventually, as a result of the Moorish conquest of Spain, some of the classic texts of Greek civilization were translated into Latin again, and gradually ancient culture was reintroduced into Europe from the 13th century.

Europe and Christianity had to wait more than a thousand years for this re-translation. The light of the Renaissance marked the birth of modern Europe when some of what had been lost during the early centuries of Christianity was rediscovered.

As J. A. Symonds put it, the "word Renaissance really means new birth to liberty – the spirit of mankind recovering consciousness . . . recognizing the beauty of the outer world . . . liberating the reason in science, and the conscience in religion".

With this rediscovery the gloomy doctrines of the end of the world, of Judgement and damnation were seen from a different perspective, as part of a much wider horizon of belief. Gradually people became aware of the vast literature of the ancient world which supported myriad ideas and speculations about the place of man in the cosmos.

Much of the early Gnostic writings, however, did not become available until the 19th century (see panel). Even when these texts were discovered, and were proved beyond a shadow of doubt to be genuine, they were reserved for study by scholars and did not become widely available to the general public. Christianity and the establishment continued the great cover-up, even though many of the texts discovered dated from closer to the time of Christ than those that are officially recognized as forming part of the Bible.

The fourth-century Gnostic, Archon

RECOVERING THE LOST SECRETS OF THE GNOSTICS

Much of the Gnostic writing was suppressed by the early Christian Fathers. Once it was decided to brand Gnosticism as a heresy, its texts were ruthlessly destroyed. Although some texts came to light in Luxor in 1769, discovered by the Scottish traveller James Bruce, and in 1773 on a London bookstall, it was not until 1851 that one of the greatest Gnostic texts, the "Pistis Sophia" was actually published.

"The Apocalypse of Peter", the "Gospel of Peter" and one of the three "Books of Enoch" were unearthed in the tomb of Akhmim in upper Egypt in 1884. These were followed in 1896/7 by the "Gospel of Mary" and the "Gospel of Thomas".

In 1945 an Arab peasant, intent upon murdering an enemy, found the Nag Hammadi codexes, regarded as the single most important source of Gnostic writings ever to have been uncovered. It has taken scholars over 45 years to make these fully available to the general reading public in English.

Bruce, discoverer of "Pistis Sophia"

Snake Worship and the Flying Magus

As Christianity evolved it taught its followers that they could be saved by their belief in God, or by the intervention of a saint or Jesus Christ on their behalf.

The astral body leaves the sleeping physical body in sleep and at death

Gnostic Christians thought that people are largely masters of their own destiny, spiritual or temporal. After death, the Gnostics believed, the soul rises from the body through various heavens. The point it reaches in this hierarchy depends on the dead person's level of spiritual knowledge and awareness. Although now denied, multiple heavens once formed a central part of Christian doctrine. In the second Corinthians 12:2, for example, Paul speaks of "such an one caught up to the third heaven".

The Gnostic Christian belief also encompassed the notion of man's soul travelling from his body during sleep, exploring even the heavens before returning to the body. In Corinthians again Paul writes, "I knew a man in Christ [i.e. a believing Christian] above fourteen years ago (whether in the body, I cannot tell; or whether out of the body, I cannot tell: God knoweth)".

Philo of Alexandria refers to a ladder of words or "Names stretching from Earth to Heaven" where the ultimate Word, the Logos, resides. At each level the soul is confronted by guardians who will not admit him to that particular heaven if he does not have the necessary purity or spiritual knowledge to gain admission. The Gnostic rises from one heaven to the next because he knows the secrets of the Spheres and their guardians.

By the late 2nd century such practices had been purged from the canon of "acceptable" Christianity. Irenaeus, Bishop of Lyons at this time, spoke disparagingly of Gnostic knowledge: "They [the Gnostic Christians] use magic and images and incantations

Simon Magus and the Emperor Nero

and invocations, and after inventing certain names as if they belonged to angels, they proclaim that some are in the first heaven, others in the second, and then try to set forth the names, principalities, angels and powers of the . . . heavens."

Irenaeus perhaps was not aware of the fact that no less a person than St Paul had given similar instructions in his own Apocalypse.

The Samarian-born Simon Magus (15 BC–AD 53), son of a Jewish sorcerer, was educated in the cradle of Gnosticism, Alexandria. He was a disciple of Dositheus, who had been a follower of John the Baptist and contended with Jesus Christ for the title of Messiah. Simon travelled widely in Persia, Arabia, Egypt to learn all he could about magical lore. He was accompanied by a sorceress called Helena, whom Simon claimed was a reincarnation of Helen of Troy. In Samaria, even Christians spoke of Simon as "the great power of God", and Peter, fearing the competition, had refused to baptize him.

Simon Magus performed many miracles, including healing the sick, raising the dead, walking through fire, flying through the air, turning stones into bread, creating phantom banquets, making himself invisible, animating stone statues, changing his own shape and, of course, reputedly commanding elemental spirits or possibly demons to do his bidding.

Clement of Alexandria called Magus the "Standing One", perhaps a discreet reference to his phallic rites with Helen, which he used to generate the necessary power for his magic. He also used the resultant semen, and Helen's menstrual blood, in his rites.

In Rome the old rivalry with the apostle Peter resulted in Simon challenging him to a demonstration of magical skill before the Roman emperor. Simon levitated and hovered while Peter kneeled and prayed hard. Peter's prayers must have been answered because Simon fell and broke his thigh, fairly conclusive proof that the Samarian had actually levitated.

SNAKE WORSHIPPERS

Animal-headed demon guardians

According to the Ophites, an early Gnostic sect, there were seven obstructive animal demons barring the soul's way to the Lesser Heavens. The names of the first four were Michael (a lion), Souriel (a bull), Raphael (a hissing snake) and Gabriel (an eagle).

Three of these are immediately recognizable as the beasts guarding the throne of God in the Apocalypse of St John: "and the first beast was like a lion, and the second beast like a calf, and the third beast had a face as a man, and the fourth beast was like a flying eagle" (5:7).

The odd one out between these two sets is, of course, the snake/man. The Ophites held the snake to be holy. This creature also represented a very special part of man. The Ophites (derived from "ophis", Greek for serpent) were in a way the predecessors of the mid-West American fundamentalist snake-handling congregations.

The three animal demons making up the seven are Thauthabaoth (a bear), Erataoth (a dog or ape, like the Egyptian god Thoth) and Oneol or Thartharoath (an ass). There may also be a correspondence between these and the Beasts that rule the world close to the millennium. As the Beast whose number is 666 has the feet of a bear (13:2), and the Beast on which the Whore of Babylon rides (17:3) is related to the ass, this seems very likely.

Nag Hammadi Cover-up

In December 1945 books containing many secrets of the Christian religion came into the hands of Mohammed 'Ali al-Samman, an Arab peasant, near the town of Nag Hammadi in upper Egypt.

Undisturbed since their concealment almost two thousand years ago, the manuscripts that were found near Nag Hammadi rank in importance with the Dead Sea Scrolls. The relatively uncorrupted texts cover the periods immediately before and after the lifetime of Christ.

What is perhaps even more extraordinary is the time it has taken scholars to make both of these very important collections of documents available in English. The first extensive translation into English did not appear until 1977. The managing editor in charge of the project said that "the publication of the tractates has encountered a number of obstacles of a political and scholarly sort. As a result, though it has been some thirty-two years since their discovery, the Nag Hammadi tractates have not previously been available in their entirety in . . . any . . . modern language".

Of the 13 codexes remaining, a total of 53 separate works have been identified, written on over 1000 sheets of papyrus – we can only guess at how much more material might have been made available had Mohammed's resourceful mother not used it as kindling (see panel).

Among these 53 works are some of the early Gospels, including secret Gospels which were not preserved in the New Testament, Greek writings and philosophy such as portions of Plato's "Republic", cosmology, poems, mystical exercises, sexual magical techniques, Jewish merkaba (chariot) mysticism, hermetic tracts and no less than five separate Apocalypses.

The Apocalypse of Paul is an account of the apostle's ascent into Heaven and what he found there, with instructions for other souls on how to conduct themselves during Judgement.

The First Apocalypse of James contains the secret teachings of Christ that were given to James the Just, his brother. In it James refers to Jesus as "Rabbi", or teacher, not God. Jesus warns James to leave Jerusalem, for the city is a dwelling place of a great number of archons (wicked or evil angels or aeons).

Jerusalem is tellingly stigmatized as the city which "always gives the cup of bitterness to the sons of light". Jesus coaches James on what to say when he is judged and challenged by the "toll collectors" of heaven in order to pass through the gates of heaven – remember, this was written before St Peter was given that job!

Less interesting are the Second Apocalypse of James and the Apocalypse of Adam, although both stress the secret knowledge of the Gnostics whose thinking made up the original

The martyrdom of St James, whose Apocalypse contains secret teachings of Christ

Christian doctrine until the Church fathers decided to become the sole dispensers of grace and knowledge.

The Apocalypse of Peter is a record of the vision of St Peter, in which he speaks with Christ in the spirit. In this Peter is clearly seen as the true successor to Christ and the founder of the Gnostic community. In the vision, Peter first sees hostile priests who seem to be intent upon stoning him and Christ to death.

Next, Peter recalls the crucifixion during which Jesus stood nearby talking with him. Peter asks, "Who is this one glad and laughing on the tree [cross]? And is it another one whose feet and hands they are striking?" Christ replies, "He whom you saw on the tree [cross], glad and laughing, this is the living Jesus. But this one into whose hands and feet they drive the nails is his fleshy part, which is the substitute being put to shame, the one who came into being in his likeness. But look at him and me."

This version of the crucifixion is obviously rather discomforting to a Church whose doctrines about the central event of Christian faith have changed considerably during the intervening centuries. It is not so surprising therefore that even in this relatively free age some pressure was exerted to keep their secret a little longer.

Peter seemed to realize that it would be a long time before his book was read and understood, for he writes "These things, then, which you saw you shall present to those of another race who are not of this age." He seems to be right, as this Apocalypse has only just seen the light of day before we enter the new age.

In the vision hostile priests wanted to stone Christ and the disciples to death

THE DISCOVERY OF THE MANUSCRIPTS

Shortly before Mohammed 'Ali al-Samman and his brothers avenged their father's murder in a blood feud, hacking off the limbs of their enemy, they went with their camels to the Jabal al-Tarif mountain near the village of Nag Hammadi to dig for "sabakh", a soft soil they used as fertilizer for their crops. The mountain was honeycombed with caves, some of which had been used as grave sites for over 4000 years. While they were digging round a massive boulder, they came across a red earthenware "Ali Baba"-type jar two or three feet high. It was carefully sealed.

At first they thought they had found one of those jars in which Solomon or some other magician used in past ages to imprison a jinn or genie. Their fear of releasing such a being was very real and was only overcome by the thought that the jar might contain gold. Taking his courage in both hands, Mohammed raised his pick and smashed the jar. Imagine their disappointment when out tumbled some 13 papyrus books bound in leather.

The brothers took the papyrus volumes home and dumped them next to the oven. Mohammed's mother burned much of the papyrus in the oven along with straw to warm the house. The family sold the surviving codexes (books) for a very small sum, not realizing that into their hands had fallen one of the largest arsenals of "spiritual dynamite" the world has seen since the establishment of Christianity.

Neoplatonism

After Christ's death Christianity settled down to a long uphill struggle against the well-established pagan cults. By AD 50 it was established in Rome, but it was not until AD 313 that it became the official religion of the Empire.

Iamblichus of Chalcis, the magician who explained how to invoke the gods

In the course of the struggle to establish Christianity over paganism some strange doctrines emerged, many of them taken from the literate Greeks who swelled the ranks of Christianity in its infancy. The Neoplatonists are an interesting example of this Christian borrowing from Greek culture.

Plutarch (AD 46–120), one of the leading Neoplatonic philosophers, lamented the passing of the old oracles and explained why he thought these had declined both in number and quality. He knew that daemons (not the same as demons) and other spiritual beings inhabited the earth along with man and the animals, something that has long since been forgotten by the majority of people.

He explained that these spiritual beings think so intensely that they produce vibrations in the air which enable other spiritual beings as well as highly sensitive men and women to receive their thoughts. This is how Plutarch explained clairvoyance and prophecy. Magicians can similarly influence the thoughts of sensitive men and women.

In as much as the daemons were not gods the information that prophets picked up from daemons sometimes turned out to contain only a grain of truth. In his book *On the Cessation of Oracles*, Plutarch explained that, unlike the gods, who are immortal, daemons do grow old and eventually die, although perhaps only after many centuries. This is how he explained the fact that the great oracles of the ancient world were by this time declining; these daemons were then very old and dying. For centuries after the advent of their religion, Christians continued to believe in the power of pagan gods, who in those days were clearly differentiated from evil spirits.

The philosopher who is usually looked upon as the founding father or codifier of Neoplatonism was Plotinus (AD 204–270). He was looked upon by his followers as divinely inspired (see panel) and by some of his detractors as an enemy of astrology.

Porphyry (AD 233–305) was a pupil of Plotinus. His books include many on magic and some 15 books devoted to attacking Christian doctrine, including the Christian view of the second coming of Christ. One of his works, a criticism of the Book of Daniel, was publicly burned by the Emperor Theodosius.

From surviving quotations we know that Porphyry declared the Book of Daniel to be the work of a Palestinian Jew, written in Greek in the period 175–64 BC. According to Porphyry, the predictions in the book correspond too exactly to events and therefore must have been written in retrospect. This is the highest tribute anyone could pay to a work of prophecy, but does not satisfactorily explain the prophecies that came true after the date of composition.

An opposing view to that put forward by Porphyry is that the Book of Daniel was actually written during the Babylonian captivity, as the text states, a dating which corresponds to its inclusion in the canon which contains no work more recent than 400 BC. The Book of Daniel was written in both Hebrew and Aramaic, but not Greek. In addition, Jesus specifically recommended it as a work of true prophecy, and he should have been in a position to know.

The Syrian Iamblichus (d. AD 333), who shared some of Porphyry's views, transformed Neoplatonism from theoretical and religious speculation into a system of magic. He explained specific procedures handed down from the ancient Greeks which were in turn passed on to seers like Nostradamus, enabling them to see into the future centuries with clarity.

Neither Porphyry nor Iamblichus used the word "magic", but spoke instead about theurgy in terms that mystics usually reserve for worship. These Neoplatonists, like the Gnostics, went into considerable detail over the use of talismans, seals, spells, invocations (for angels and guardians of the gates of the lower heavens) and evocations (for demonic manifestations). They developed a religious approach to the techniques of the magicians which were so important to pseudo-messiahs like Simon Magus.

The idea of hierarchies of spiritual and demonic beings was also introduced into the theology of Christianity, although the magical techniques which were part and parcel of them were rigorously suppressed. This suppression sparked off a battle that would run for centuries, a war ostensibly between the forces of good and evil but in reality a continuation of the conflict between paganism and its usurper, Christianity.

Spirits of the Moon, Mercury and Venus

INVOKING THE DAEMON

The Neoplatonist Plotinus maintained that only the physical and irrational side of man's nature was affected by either drugs or sorcery. The rational soul, he declared, may free itself from the influence of magic.

Nevertheless, an Egyptian priest had little difficulty in persuading Plotinus to allow him to demonstrate his magical powers by invoking his familiar daemon. Plotinus, who had by this time been living and teaching in Rome for 26 years, decided that the only pure place in the city for the priest to undertake his experiment was in the Temple of Isis.

One evening the two men went to the temple with some friends of Plotinus, and set about the invocation. Instead of a daemon or guardian spirit appearing, a god materialized. One can imagine the impact this made on the assembled group. Given the spiritual standing of Plotinus, however, perhaps a god was only to be expected.

Secrets of the Ten Heavens

A large number of the books in the New Testament were written by the Apostle Paul. The manuscripts of several of these have only recently come to light.

"The Apocalypse of Paul" was discovered in December 1945, together with a number of other manuscripts, near the village of Nag Hammadi in Egypt. This work outlines the early Gnostic Christian idea of what happens after death, when the soul is judged.

According to Paul's Apocalypse, each soul has to rise as best it can through a hierarchy of heavens and face the increasingly difficult challenges posed by the guardian angels of each heaven. The book focuses on Paul's ascent to the tenth and highest heaven. The journey begins with Paul meeting a child on the mountain of Jericho, on the way to heaven (symbolized by Jerusalem). This child turns out to be the Holy Spirit, who takes Paul first to the third heaven.

The Holy Spirit warns Paul to keep his wits about him, for they are about to enter the realm of "principalities . . . archangels and powers and the whole race of demons". The Holy Spirit also mentions that they will pass "one that reveals bodies to a soul-seed", that is, the being that takes souls and plants them in new bodies for reincarnation.

The vision of St Paul

For the soul who wished to ascend to the highest heaven, reincarnation was to be avoided. This was part of Christian doctrine until AD 553, when it was suppressed.

When Paul reaches the fourth heaven, the Holy Spirit encourages him to look down upon his body which he has left behind on the mountain of Jericho. As Paul ascends he witnesses in the fourth heaven the judgement and punishment of another soul. He says, "I saw the angels resembling gods . . . bringing a soul out of the land of the dead". The soul has been resurrected so that it can be judged, one of the four events promised for the end of the world. The angels were whipping it, a scene which clashes with the sugar-sweet angels depicted by Victorian Christians!

The soul spoke, saying, "What sin was it that I committed in the world?" The "toll collector" of this heavenly gate accuses the soul. The soul replies, "Bring witnesses! Let them [show] you in what body I committed lawless deeds". Three bodies rise up as witnesses and accuse the soul of anger and envy, and finally murder. "When the soul heard these things, it gazed downwards in sorrow . . . It was cast down."

At this point we expect the soul to be cast into hell, as in later Christian doctrine, but no: "the soul that had been cast down [went] to [a] body which had been prepared [for it]", and was reincarnated.

Paul, somewhat shaken by this experience, was beckoned forward by the Holy Spirit and allowed to pass through the gate of the fifth heaven. Here he saw his fellow apostles, and "a great angel in the fifth heaven holding an iron rod in his hand". This angel and three other angels, with whips in their hands, scourge the souls of the dead and drive them on to judgement. Paul remains with the Holy Spirit and the gates to the sixth heaven swing open effortlessly before him.

SECRET SPIRITUAL KNOWLEDGE

One of the Heavens from the Last Judgement

It is not surprising that the early Christian fathers edited out the practical spiritual knowledge which was once an integral part of Christianity, and was known and practised by the Apostle Paul. For these men, it was far more convenient and gratifying for their egos to assert that spiritual grace could only be attained through them as Christ's representatives on Earth. In a move that is very unlikely to have met with the approval of Jesus Christ himself, the worldly aspirations of a few won out over the spiritual enlightenment of the many.

As we approach the end of the millennium, when some expect the Apocalypse to become a reality, it is only fitting that this early spiritual dimension should be fully recognized and understood. After 2000 years of silence, the essence of Paul's early teaching again became available to us just 23 years before the end of the millennium.

Ironically, the Second Coming, or reincarnation, awaited with such relish by some zealots may be viewed as proof of God's imperfection rather than of his omnipotence. According to Paul, reincarnation was the lot of any-one who failed to scale the heights of the ten heavens.

In the sixth heaven Paul sees a strong light shining down on him from the heaven above. He is motioned by the "toll collector" through the gates of the seventh heaven. Here, he sees "an old man [filled with] light [and whose garment] was white. [His throne], which is in the seventh heaven, [was] brighter than the sun by [seven] times." This old man bears a striking resemblance to Jehovah as he is described in the vision of Ezekiel.

The old man asks, "Where are you going, Paul?" Only reluctantly, after some encouragement from the Holy Spirit, does Paul speak with him and give the Gnostic sign he has learned. The eighth heaven then opens and Paul ascends. Here he embraces the twelve disciples, most of whom he has not met before, and together they rise to the ninth heaven. Finally, Paul reaches the tenth and highest heaven, where he is transformed.

Sorcerers, SPIRITS & SCRYERS

History was seen as a progression through various ages, governed by angels, culminating in the end of the world and the rule of Christ on Earth. Scryers called upon the angels to divulge the secrets of the future, and the Pope elected to rule the Church on the last day of the first millennium was a well known sorcerer.

Gerbert and the First Millennium

Towards the close of the first millennium, in AD 999, many Christians in Europe thought that the world was coming to an end, and that Christ's Second Coming was at hand.

The first millennium pope Sylvester II was rumoured to be a sorcerer

For a few short months in AD 999 people could talk of nothing else but the Second Coming. The pope who reigned at the end of the first millennium was one of the most fascinating and mysterious personalities in papal history. After the death of Pope Gregory V at the tender age of 27 (by poison, according to rumour) a scholarly prelate called Gerbert was chosen to occupy the throne of St Peter as Pope Sylvester II.

Gerbert, the first Frenchman to become Pope, was from a humble home in Aurillac in the Auvergne region. Tradition has it that he was an advanced student of the black arts, which he first learnt during three years in residence at certain Arabic schools in Spain. It was said that he regularly conversed with the Devil, and was even thought by some cardinals to be the cloven-hoofed Devil himself.

The official version of the background of the shepherd charged to usher the Catholic flock into the second millennium was, of course, slightly different. This emphasized his devotion to mathematics and the natural sciences which in those days were largely overlapping disciplines, particularly in the popular imagination. Gerbert taught grammar, dialectic, rhetoric, arithmetic, music, astronomy and geometry and supported the classics as an essential part of education. Like Friar Bacon, he was credited with possessing a "brazen head" which spoke to him and could prophesy future events.

As the first year of Gerbert's papacy approached the millennial hour, his parishioners in Germanic and Slav countries expected the world to end in fire. In the countries bordering on the

Mediterranean, meanwhile, the most popular vision was of a great blast on Gabriel's trumpet summoning the dead from their graves to share in the Last Judgement with "the quick", those who had not yet died.

In Europe generally a sort of mass hysteria progressively took hold as the year end approached. This atmosphere led to some astonishing happenings. Some men forgave each other their debts; husbands and wives rashly confessed their infidelities; convicts were released from prison; poachers made a truce with their liege lords; fields were left fallow, and buildings went unrepaired by their owners. After all, their reasoning ran, why repair a building that will not be needed in a few months' time? In direct obedience to the Bible, some of the more pious rich gave their surplus vestments to the poor, although keeping their best for that all-important meeting with their divine maker. More mercenary souls went round snapping up property at knock-down prices. Many people were convinced by the argument that, in a world with no future, such possessions were worthless.

The confessionals did a roaring trade as people put their spiritual life in order to stake a claim in the afterlife as best they could. The demand for absolution almost outstripped the ability of the priests to physically give it, so great was the rush, and general absolutions were celebrated in special masses. Many who had lived in sin promptly got married. Huge bands of pilgrims set out for the Holy Land with the hope of arriving in time to meet Christ in Jerusalem. On the road they either whipped themselves as penitents, or

sang hymns, while at night they scanned the heavens for the signs of His coming.

December saw fanaticism reach new heights as communities attempted to rid their area of the ungodly so that the Angel of Judgement would not need to call: bands of flagellants roamed the countryside; mobs called for the execution of suspected sorcerers or unpopular burghers, and even some farm animals were freed to roam through the towns, giving a slightly surrealistic air to the proceedings.

On the night of 31 December, Gerbert celebrated mass in the Basilica of St Peter's in Rome. The packed congregation believed this might be the last mass they would ever attend. When the mass had been said, a deathly silence fell over the congregation – but they waited in vain.

Life soon resumed its usual pace. Perhaps the only people not disappointed were those who knew they would never have made it through St Peter's gates, and those who had gained at the expense of the gullible.

WHAT GERBERT LEARNED FROM THE MOORS

According to the 12th-century historian William of Malmesbury, Gerbert fled by night from his monastery to Spain to study astrology and "the other arts with the Saracens". The Muslim invaders of Spain had at that time reached a higher level of civilization than Christian northern Europe. Under Muslim tuition, Gerbert learned "what the song and flight of birds portend [augury], to summon ghostly figures from the lower world [necromancy], and whatever human curiosity has encompassed whether harmful or salutary" [other arts and sciences].

Michael Scott, referring to him as Master Gilbertus, claims he was the best "nigromancer" (necromancer or magician) in France, "whom the demons obeyed in all that he required of them day and night, because of the great sacrifices which he offered, and his prayers and

fastings and magic books and great diversity of rings and candles".

Given this background, it is not surprising that Gerbert was regarded by his contemporaries as the best man for the job of Pope at the end of the world.

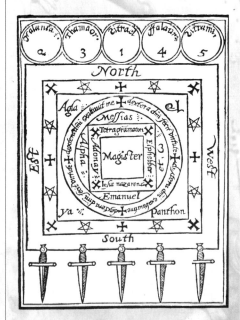

Circle for binding spirits in a crystal

The Apocalypse of Joachim

The classic apocalyptic prophecy of the 13th century was produced by Joachim of Fiore (1145–1202), abbot of Cortale in the Italian province of Calabria, who was asked by three popes to write a work on the Apocalypse.

Joachim's response was *Expositio in Apocalypsin*. He divided history up into three periods, with each period prefaced by a time of incubation. Joachim's idea is very similar to that behind the Astrological Ages.

Joachim describes how while meditating one Easter night he became aware of a stream of bright light pouring into his soul. The meaning of the Apocalypse was laid open to him. He prophesied the advent of the Antichrist, and informed Richard Coeur de Lion, when he came to consult him, that the Antichrist would soon occupy the Papal throne itself. Joachim said that the Papacy would be stripped of all temporal power, a prediction that was not to come true for another six centuries, in 1870.

Joachim's book provoked much speculation about the arrival of the millennium, a topic for discussion which St Augustine had desperately tried to discourage during his lifetime. The kingdom of God, Augustine said repeatedly, had already arrived. In the half-century after Joachim's death, *Expositio* was revered as a new eschatology beside that contained in the Book of Daniel, the Apocalypse of St John the Divine and the forged Sibylline Oracles.

Let us now look at Joachim's three ages of history.

The first Age was the Age of the Father, the age of the Mosaic Law of the Old Testament.

The second Age was the Age of the Son, during which the Gospel of the New Testament held sway. Both these Ages had already run their course, and Joachim claimed to be living in the incubation period of the third Age. This was to usher in the Age of the Paraclete or Holy Spirit, which was to begin at some time between 1200 and 1260, and would endure until the millennium and the Last Judgement.

The first Age was one of fear and servitude, the second one of faith and brotherly submission, and the third Age, Joachim predicted, would be one of love, joy and freedom, with spiritual

St Augustine heralded the Third Age

knowledge revealed directly into the hearts of men.

Joachim expected that there would arise a new teacher, a new Elias or *novus dux* who, like Christ, would have 12 apostles who would form a new order of monks. Another figure expected before the end was the first Antichrist, who most authorities are agreed should be described as an ordinary ruler with extraordinary powers. His reign would last only three and a half years, but in that period he would overthrow the Church and expel the Pope. This parallels the vision of a 20th-century Pope who saw his successor being forced out of the Vatican.

After the overthrow of the Antichrist there would be a period of universal peace. This would precede the natural disasters and upheavals heralding the coming of a second Antichrist, followed soon after by the Last Judgement.

One ruler became an almost mythical figure thanks to Joachim. The Holy Roman Emperor Frederick II (1194–1250), who was excommunicated at least three times for perjury, blasphemy and heresy, was thought by his enemies to be the Antichrist. But his supporters saw him as the Emperor of the Last Days or the *novus dux* written about by Joachim.

During the Crusades, Frederick captured Jerusalem, Bethlehem and Nazareth from the Muslims, together with part of what is now Lebanon. He was crowned King of Jerusalem, and it was whispered that he had come to claim the city for Christ's impending descent to Earth. For his followers, Frederick's success in the Crusades confirmed his status of near-divinity.

When Frederick died in 1250, his supporters fully expected him to rise from the grave and lead them once again. As Joachim's deadline for the unfurling of the Age of the Spirit, 1260, approached, so-called "armies of saints" took to flagellating themselves in public, with the aim of avoiding much greater punishments on the approaching Day of Judgement. The famine in 1258 and plague in 1259 lent credibility to 1260 as the correct millennial date, but the year came and went and life carried on as normal.

In the third century armies of saints took to flagellation to expiate their sins

THE TABLES OF THE LAW

The Irish poet W. B. Yeats mentions in his *Mythologies* a little-known book of Joachim's entitled *Liber Inducens in Evangelium Aeternum*. Yeats wondered if the book was perhaps just "some mediaeval straw-splitting . . .which is only useful today to show how many things are unimportant to us, which once shook the world".

After reading Joachim's book, Yeats wrote of his experience: "the dust shall fall for many years over this little box [the book was kept in a box made by the Renaissance gold-smith, Benvenuto Cellini]; and then I shall open it; and the tumults which are, perhaps, the flames of the Last Day shall come from under the lid". Yeats' poetic vision also looked to the end of this century for the Second Coming of Christ.

Another of Joachim's books, *Adversus Judaeos* ("Against the Jews") propounded the argument that while all Jews will be finally converted to Christianity in the last days, they will before then follow the Antichrist (in company with a large number of Christians) and bring great suffering upon themselves and the whole world.

To avoid this fate, Joachim urged the conversion of the Jews before the appearance of the Antichrist. His suggestion would later cause a lot of grief and hatred, although his intention had been well-meaning and anticipated a much purer millennial Age of joy and brotherly love.

The Abbot Trithemius

Prophecies of events and of the angelic rulers of the world through to the year AD 2233 were made in 1508 by Trithemius, a master of cryptography and magic.

Trithemius, master of the angels

The turn of the 16th century was a strange time. Columbus had just discovered America by accident while making his way to China and the East. The Pope was the corrupt and worldly Rodrigo Borgia (Alexander VI), who inhabited the Vatican between 1492 and 1503 with his mistress Venozza Catanei and his four children. It was no secret that he had secured his election by paying enormous bribes to the other cardinals. Borgia lived like a decadent pagan emperor, with all that entailed, including orgies, and was hardly plausible as the representative of Christ on earth.

At this time was born the mysterious Johannes Trithemius (1462–1516), a man who could speak with the angels and send messages long distances in the twinkling of an eye, almost four centuries before the invention of the telephone. A brilliant scholar and teacher of two of the greatest commentators on and practitioners of European magic of the period, Cornelius Agrippa and Paracelsus, Trithemius was appointed Abbot of Sponheim at the incredibly young age of 23. Trithemius was also interested in "magical alphabets" and was in a sense the father of cryptography, the science of writing secret messages in code. Some of his methods of code writing were used by John Dee, a spy for Queen Elizabeth I.

Prophecies made by Trithemius are recorded in a very strange little book entitled *De Septem Secundeis, id est, Intelligentiis, sive Spiritibus Orbes post Deum moventibus*, or "Of the Seven Spirits, or heavenly Intelligences governing the Orbs [of the Planets] under God's Rule". Despite the obscure title, the book clearly explains an elaborate system of cycles of time, and a succession of angels who govern these cycles.

Trithemius gives the whole history of the world from the Creation to the end of time. He divides this massive spectrum into Ages, each made up of chunks of 354 years and four months. Each Age is ruled over by an Angel. The first in the sequence is Orisiel (reporting to Saturn), who is followed by Anael (Venus), then Zachariel (Jupiter), Raphael (Mercury), Samael

Seven angels representing Trithemius' seven cyclical ages

(Mars), Gabriel (the Moon) and, finally, Michael (the Sun).

The first Age, from the Creation, which according to Trithemius began on 15 March, is ruled over by Orisiel. During the period of his reign, Trithemius notes, "men were rude, and did cohabit together in desert and uncouth places, after the homely manner of Beasts".

Leon Trotsky was born under Michael

From Anno Mundi 354 to Anno Mundi 708 (calculating from Creation), Anael, under the influence of Venus, encouraged men to build houses and erect cities, create clothes and develop the arts of spinning and weaving. The influence of Venus made man wanton, and as a consequence men "took unto themselves faire women for their wives, [and] neglected God".

Trithemius himself lived in the nineteenth Age when the world was ruled for the third time by Samael, representing Mars, the god of war. His rule extended from the year 6378, measured in years Anno Mundi (since the Creation, otherwise known as AD 1171) until 6732 Anno Mundi (AD 1525). One of the main happenings in this period of history was the so-called Hundred Years' War between England and France.

Samael's reign was followed by that of the Angel Gabriel, ruled by the Moon, from 6732 Anno Mundi (AD 1525) until 7086 Anno Mundi (November AD 1879). In the following Age, the reins were taken over by the Angel Michael, who will hold sway until the year AD 2233. Michael was the archangel who led the forces of light to victory against the Devil in the first war in heaven.

The events of the millennium will thus be under the control of this angel of the Sun, reflecting the idea of the Second Coming, as Christ is sometimes identified with the Sun and is indeed called Michael by some commentators. It is as if Christ is to return to complete the work he began when he was on earth. Interestingly, Communist stalwarts Joseph Stalin and Leon Trotsky were both born in 1879, the beginning of the Age of the Sun.

Under the dominion of the angel Michael, "Kings began first to be amongst Mortall men", but in this reign he is concerned with the removal of as many kings as possible, so we can be sure that by the year 2233 the institution of monarchy will no longer be alive in any country.

Michael also originally presided over "the worship of several Gods", and so a revival of paganism at the end of the century is on the cards. This angel was also in at the birth of the sciences of mathematics, astronomy

TRITHEMIUS THE SORCERER

Trimethius' ability as a sorcerer is demonstrated by the feat he performed for the German Emperor Maximilian I in 1482. At this time Maximilian was greatly distressed by the death of his wife Maria, daughter of Charles the Bold, Duke of Burgundy. He asked Trithemius to call up her shade or spirit.

Trithemius did so, and although the Emperor was not permitted to speak with the vision that appeared before him, so complete was the materialization that the Emperor recognized a wart upon its neck, which convinced him that it was indeed the spirit of his Empress. This episode in Trithemius' life has become part of the legends that were later associated with Faust.

and magic. Appropriately, Albert Einstein, the prize-winning physicist, was born in that key year, 1879, the opening year of Michael's Age.

Mathematics and astronomy have taken great strides in the first two thirds of Michael's reign. A revival in that third art, magic, is on the cards for the last third of his reign, starting in the year 2115.

By placing Michael last in the cycle of angels, Trithemius was indicating that this reign would see the end of the world. If you accept his prophecy, this will not arrive earlier than AD 2233.

St Malachy

Time has proved wrong the many people who originally dismissed the prophecies of St Malachy as a hoax.

Did St Bernard of Clairvaux know the secrets of St Malachy's clairvoyance?

The passage of time has proved doubters of St Malachy wrong, for his prophecies have turned out to be amazingly accurate. He even prophesied the precise date of his own death, and got it right. The prophecies concern the papacy, starting with Pope Celestine II in 1143. In all, 112 popes and their characteristics are listed from 1143 "to the end of the world"!

Maelmhaedhoc O'Morgair (later Latinized to Malachy) was born in Armagh in 1094. He became Archbishop of Armagh in 1132, dying on All Souls' Day 1148 in the arms of his French biographer to be, St Bernard of Clairvaux.

When making his prophecies Malachy usually encapsulated the pope's name, family background or coat of arms. The heraldic coat of arms was either of the pope's family or that given to him when he ascended to the papacy. For example, Pope Alexander VII (1655–67) had a family coat of arms showing three hills with a star shining above them: Malachy calls him *Montium Custos* or "the Guardian of the Hills". That of Leo XIII (1878–1903) depicted a golden comet on an azure field, which Malachy foreshadowed with his tag *Lumen in Coelo*, or "a Light in the Sky".

Sometimes the personal history of the pope plays a part in the motto given by Malachy. Clement XIII (1758–69), who had connections with the government of the Italian state of Umbria and whose emblem was a rose, was called by Malachy *Rosa Umbriae*, the "Rose of Umbria".

In our own century, Benedict XV (1914–22), who was indicated by Malachy as *Religio Depopulata*

("Religion Depopulated"), reigned in a time which saw the founding of Communism, an anti-religious movement if ever there was one, and the rapid reduction of intense religious belief. His successor, Pius XI (1922–39), truly lived up to his motto of *Fides Intrepida* ("Unshaken Faith"), speaking out against both Hitler and Mussolini and denouncing Communism. *Pius Angelicus*, the "Angelic Shepherd", was an apt description of Eugenio Pacelli, who wore the papal hat as Pope Pius XII.

The election of *Pastor et Nauta* ("Shepherd and Sailor") brought a touch of farce to the election process. It is said, on flimsy evidence, that while the conclave to elect the pope was being held in Rome, Cardinal Spellman of New York attempted to fulfil Malachy's prophecy by hiring a boat filled with sheep and sailing it up and down the River Tiber. Giuseppe Roncalli was eventually appointed, his elevation from the See of Venice (symbolized by the sailor) to the papacy (symbolized by the shepherd) amply vindicating Malachy's motto.

This pope was succeeded by Paul VI (1963–78), whose coat of arms was three fleurs-de-lys, Malachy's *Flos Florum* ("Flower of Flowers"). The next pope was John Paul I, whose real name, Albino Luciani, means "pale light". His birthplace, Belluno (beautiful moon), was identified by Malachy as *De Medietate Lunae*, or "Of the Half [or middle of the] Moon".

The present incumbent, John Paul II, is the former Archbishop of Krakow, Karol Wojtyla. He was born on the day of a solar eclipse (18 May 1920) and once laboured in a quarry in his native Poland. In Malachy's prophecies he is referred to as "De Labore Solis".

According to Malachy, there are only two more popes to come before the end of the world. Significantly, the last pope will have the same name as the first shepherd of the Roman Catholic Church, the apostle Peter. Malachy refers to this second Peter as "Petrus Romanus" ("Peter of Rome"), and he has more to say about him than any of the other pontiffs. His prophecy is unequivocal. This Peter "will feed his flock among many tribulations; after which the seven-hilled city will be destroyed and the dreadful Judge will judge the people."

It is clear from this that Pope Peter will preside over the end of the Roman Catholic Church, which will suffer persecution, perhaps at the hands of the Antichrist. The word "tribulation" is commonly used to describe the immediate pre-millennium period. The seven-hilled city is obviously Rome itself. The "dreadful Judge" may well be a reference to Christ, who will come to sit at the right hand of God the Father to judge the living and the dead.

THE POPE IN A TRANCE

Further confirmation of the end of the Roman Catholic Church was given to Pope Pius X (1835–1914) in 1909 in a vision. During an audience with the General Chapter of the Franciscans, Pius fell into a semi-trance and sat with his head sunk upon his chest. After a few minutes he came to and opened his eyes, a look of horror etched on his face. He cried out:

"What I have seen was terrible ... Will it be myself? Will it be my successor? What is certain is that the pope will quit Rome, and in fleeing from the Vatican he will have to walk over the dead bodies of his priests. Do not tell anyone while I am alive."

In times of trouble the pope could leave the Vatican for the relative safety of the castle of St Angelo via a causeway high above street level. This was not part of the vision, so it is likely that the pope Pius saw was fleeing from more than a temporary danger. In Pius's lifetime Communism was identified as the greatest enemy of Catholicism, and it was a takeover by such a secular force that Pius most feared. But who is to say that what he really saw was not the departure of the last pope, as foretold by Malachy?

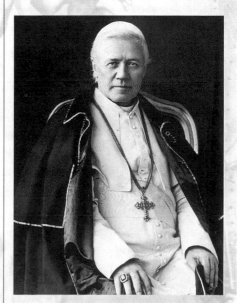

Pope Pius X

The Year of the Beast: 1666

A favourite for the accolade of Apocalypse year was 1666. It had been chosen because it represented the sum of the first millennium (1000) plus the number of the Beast recorded in the Apocalypse of St John (666).

In the mid 1660s the citizens of London must have thought they were indeed witnessing the end of the world: in 1665 they were ravaged by a plague which killed at least 68,000, and in the following year much of their city was destroyed by a great fire.

In the 17th century traditional sources for prophetic calculations continued to be the Bible. The most widely read prophetic source of the period was *Merlin Ambrosius*, a sort of blend of the prophecies of King Arthur's magician Merlin, the nationalist Welsh bard Myrddin, those included by Geoffrey of Monmouth in the seventh book of his *Historia Regium Britanniae* and those of Ambrosius in the *Historia Britonum of Nennius*. Also well-known were the prophecies of "Mother Shipton".

The prophecies of Merlin had been reissued in the 14th century to support the English claim to the throne of France, and in the 15th to justify the aspirations of the rival houses of York and Lancaster. Some prophecies of the Welsh Merlin lent support to the rebellions of Owain Glyndwr against Henry IV, and by Rhys ap Gruffydd against Henry VIII. Prophecy became so intertwined with rebellion that laws were brought in by the Tudors to stifle its pernicious influence.

Many of the prophets prominent in the century before the English Civil War saw themselves as playing a part in the Last Judgement and the arrival of the Kingdom of God. There was no shortage of messiahs. In the late 16th and early 17th centuries the coming apocalypse was frequently cited in the conflict between the Roman Catholic Church and Protestantism. The Puritans called the Church of Rome "the Whore of Babylon" which, according to the Bible, would be destroyed. Ironically, it was during the reign of the anti-Puritan King James I that the Bible was made available in English in a standard edition. Suddenly, many people who could not have read it before in Latin were now able to find those wonderful, stirring passages in Daniel, Ezekiel and the Apocalypse of St John which had for centuries been providing fuel for prophetic interpreters, and still do.

Some people who believed that the end was near – known as millenarians – reported visitations by prophetic messengers. William Sedgwick, preacher at Ely Cathedral, believed that Christ himself had told him that "the world will be at an end within fourteen days" and went to London to

Apocalyptic judgement was cast upon old London with the Great Fire of 1666

inform the King. The most active millenarianism occurred in the turbulent years before the rule of the Puritan Oliver Cromwell. At this time a number of pseudo-messiahs attracted followings, among them two weavers, Richard Farnham and John Bull, who in 1636 proclaimed themselves "divine witnesses" . They professed to have knowledge of things to come, and to be able to inflict plagues on their enemies if they so chose. They quoted the Apocalypse of St John 11:3: "and I will give power unto my two witnesses, and they shall prophesy a thousand two hundred and threescore days." Empowerment by the Lord did not prevent their imprisonment and subsequent executions in 1642.

Yet another messiah from this period was Edward Wightman, who claimed to be the Elias or Elijah foretold in Malachy 4:5. In 1612 he became the last Englishman to be burned for heresy. The Ranter John Robbins was deified by his followers who held his wife to be the Virgin Mary and his son Jesus: his divine mission was to carry out the conversion of the Jews and to reconnoitre Jerusalem!

From the mid 17th century prophecy and popular interest in the millennium were on the wane, certainly in England. In 1655 Meric Casuabon, in *A Treatise Concerning Enthusiasm*, declared that every case of religious ecstasy was no more than "a degree and species of epilepsy"; this from a man who had previously published the diaries of that arch seeker after divine knowledge and dealer in angelic prophecies, Dr John Dee.

In the later 17th century, when everyone had had a bellyful of

OLD MOTHER SHIPTON AND ARMAGEDDON

Mother Shipton, witch and prophetess, rides in style

Mother Shipton was one of a number of prophets – Nostradamus and the astrologer William Lilly were others – who predicted that London would be ravaged by fire. Her prophecies were first published in 1641, some 25 years before the Great Fire.

The real name of "Mother Shipton" was Ursula Southiel (1488–1561). Born at Knaresborough, Yorkshire – the result of a union between her mother and a demon, so it was claimed – she was reputed to be extraordinarily ugly, and perhaps because of this she lived in a cave for part of her life. Her most interesting prediction concerns Armageddon:

"Then shall come the Son of Man [Christ], having a fierce beast in his arms, which kingdom lies in the Land of the Moon [perhaps the Middle East], which is dreadful throughout the whole world; with a number of people shall he pass many waters and shall come to the land of the Lyon [lion, hence England]; look for help of the Beast of his country, and an Eagle [USA] shall destroy castles of the Thames, and there shall be a battle among many kingdoms . . . and therewith shall be crowned the Son of Man, and the . . . Eagles shall be preferred [by the people] and there shall be peace over the world, and there shall be plenty."

millennium predictions, it became acceptable to declare that the books of Daniel and Revelation should be read metaphorically and not literally. Even the Quakers came to accept that

prophecy was distinctly odd. Thanks to the Reformation, religion had lost its wonder-working qualities. Not until more than a century later would prophecy be taken seriously again.

The Book of Prophecies

Around AD 346 one of the most extraordinary books of prophecy, the Liber Vaticinationem Quodam Instinctumentis, *was born. Written by an unknown scholar, it is the only prophetic book to provide exact dates.*

The ill-fated Archduke Ferdinand

This book was rigorously suppressed by the Vatican, and appears to have only survived in one or two manuscript copies. One copy found its way into the huge collection of esoteric books and manuscripts amassed by the Nazis during World War II, and was stored in a warehouse in Poznan in Poland.

This manuscript probably dates from around the second half of the 16th century, and may have been made from a much earlier original. The main text is written in Latin. The manuscript divides history into a series of overlapping periods. Each of these is called a norma, Latin for "a rule, precept, model, or pattern". The normae cover fixed periods of time, usually 60 or 144 years, and the prophecies allocated to them are very precise indeed.

Liber Vaticinationem suggests that certain events cause other events to happen. If the first, precipitating, event is delayed, then the second event may not happen at all. The date at which each norma begins (its *dies natalis*) depends upon complex calculations centred on the dates of realized events in the previous normae.

Let us take a specific norma, the 63rd, and examine its prophecies. This norma is called *Nullus Modus Caedibus Fuit* which, roughly translated, means "there was no end to the slaughter". It reads:

63:1 *"This 'norma' will only be fresh born*
When none but the quarrelsome wolf
Has lifted up his arm against another
In the Empire for one hundred years."

I interpret this to cover the period 1915 to 2058. The word "Empire" indicates Europe, as defined by the Roman Empire. The prophecies predicted will take place (the norma will be born) only after a period of 100 years of relative peace in Europe. The "quarrelsome wolf" is Germany. Now, as there was a period of relative peace

***"Mighty sounds light up the nights"** – a prophecy of modern warfare?*

The German "Beast" attacks Europe

in Europe for 99 years from the defeat of Napoleon at Waterloo in 1815 until 1915 (with the exception of the Franco-Prussian War in 1870) this norma was due to begin in 1915:

63:4 *"There will be no end to the slaughter*
As the wolf from the North of Rome
Tears thrice at the body of the Empire.
Even the Eastern empire shall shake."

This seems to suggest a state of war and death caused by the wolf (Germany) attacking the rest of the Empire (Europe) three times. Even Russia (the Eastern empire) will be involved. There follows a description of each of these three wars:

63:5 *"For the first a noble is twice attacked*
In the streets of Illyria and dies.
The wolf lifts up its eyes to the moon,
And the Eastern empire loses its head."

The first war is obviously the 1914–18 conflict, with the "noble twice attacked", the Austrian Archduke Ferdinand whose assassination in Sarajevo on 28 June 1914 sparked

hostilities. There were two separate attempts to kill Ferdinand on that day.

"The wolf lifts up its eyes to the moon" refers to Germany's alliance with Turkey, represented by the crescent moon of Islam. Russia (the Eastern empire) was drawn into the war and in 1917 deposed its Tsar ("loses its head"). Verse 63:14 states "when two years of months has passed away", making an opening date for the second war at 1915 (when the norma started) plus 24 equals 1939.

63:6 *"For the second, Rome conspires with the wolf:*
Between them they eat the Empire.
Mighty sounds light up the nights
And countless multitudes trample."

The last two lines are a fairly accurate description of the fruits of World War II: aerial bombardment, forced migration, and millions of displaced persons.

63:7 *"For the third, the earth shakes*
The throat of the Gaul is ravaged
Many die fleeing from the awful winds
The sun halts in its path in the heaven."

World War III has not yet happened, but this prophecy tells us what to expect. In 63:16, we are told: "The norma will die or be completed [*vita decedere*] when the wolf is cut in two", which could refer only to the partition of Germany in 1945. This particularly violence-packed norma is succeeded by the 64th norma which, by this reckoning, covers the period 1945–2089

THE FUTURE ACCORDING TO *LIBER VATICINATIONEM*

Trying to get to the bottom of the dating of the prophecies contained in the *Liber Vaticinationem* is a bit like tackling a very difficult IQ test. Having said this, when the calculations are made correctly the book appears to provide exact dates for major events which occurred centuries after the book was written. The amazing predictions of the 63rd chapter of the manuscript are good examples. But what of the future? It is time to lift the corner of the page and glimpse the predictions which the 64th norma makes for the years 1945–2089. See what you can make of these:

64:9 *"The gods of the ancients will return*
To the streets and the taverns of the Empire.
The trees will shrivel in the hot wind
And the waters of Florence will become dry.
In the land beyond the Pillars of Hercules
There will rise the ghost of an horned image
And the prophet [haruspex] will return to the table
While the waters retreat from the hives[?].
In lowing, the cattle will bring the tiger upon them
But the stave of the farmer stays his mouth
From the country of the Jews comes quickly
The man who is justified by the horn of plenty."

Nostradamus,
PRINCE
of
PROPHETS

Mich. Nostradamus

No other prophet combined the amazingly successful techniques of the prophetesses of ancient Greece, with a deep knowledge of the Jewish Qabalah, and the mechanisms of the stars. No other prophet made predictions across such a vast timespan, and was so consistently right.

Nostradamus's Prophetic Vision

The prophet Nostradamus (1503–66) was born in Provence, France, on 14 December 1503, the son of Jewish converts.

Michel de Nostredame, the first Jewish prophet to use ancient Greek methods

Nostradamus's education embraced the classics as well as Hebrew, astrology and the Qabalah. He also read from ancient books on magic and Greek prophecy, which he later burnt. He studied philosophy at Avignon and medicine at Montpelier.

In 1555 the first of his *Centuries* were published. The complete work, issued in 1568, comprised ten groups of approximately 100 verses or quatrains, and covered the period 1555 until the end of the world, which Nostradamus prophesied would come in AD 3797. A great number of events are prophesied in the *Centuries*, sometimes in astonishing detail.

Nostradamus drew on traditional prophetic methods used by the sibyls and pythonesses of ancient Greece. He confirmed in his famous letter of 1558 to Henri II of France that he used a "tripode aeneo", brazen tripod. He also describes his gift of prophecy as "an emotion that steals over me . . . an emotional tendency handed down to me from a line of ancestors". He saw "the great events, sad or portentous" as if he were "looking into a burning mirror, as with darkened vision", like other scryers of the period such as Edward Kelley.

Nostradamus practised his prophecy at night, "at certain subsecival [leisure] hours". After foreseeing an event he would then use astrological and astronomical methods to calculate a precise date for the vision: he "calculated the present prophecies in accordance with the order of the chain which contains the revolution, and the whole by astronomical rule".

Having completed his calculations, Nostradamus would deliberately avoid including the relevant date for an event in his quatrains, even though this would have been possible: "had I wished to give every quatrain its detailed date, it could easily have been done". Irksome indeed for the student of the *Centuries* who has to be content with the meagre number of precise dates he did give – nine in the 1000 quatrains and eight in other passages. The dates have also been preserved in a few other quatrains, but concealed within astrological terminology.

In order to establish the exact dating of Nostradamus's prophecies about the Apocalypse, we must first unravel his system of dating. The first challenge is to break his dating code. Most successful systematic prophecies depend upon recurring time periods. *Liber Vaticinationem*, for example, relies upon "normae", or periods of 60 years, for its predictions.

Although it is not mentioned by any interpreter of his prophecies to date, Nostradamus used the orbits of the planets round the Sun to date the future events revealed to him. Specifically, he used those of Saturn and Jupiter, respectively 29.458 and 11.862 years. In IX:73, for example, he measures a king's reign by this method: "he will reign less than a [r]evolution of Saturn", and in the previous quatrain "Saturn two three cycles completed".

We have already examined the considerable predictive significance in the conjunction of these two planets, which are the heaviest in the solar system. Nostradamus estimated that an almost even multiple of their orbits – 60 – indicated the imminence of significant events.

NOSTRADAMUS'S SECRET CLOCK

For the ancients and Nostradamus, there were no Uranus, Neptune or Pluto beyond the planets Saturn and Jupiter to confuse the picture, as these had not yet been discovered. The orbits of the other planets (Mercury, Venus and Mars) were too rapid to use as a measure for the forthcoming centuries. Hence Jupiter and Saturn became Nostradamus's clock of the future.

Jupiter and Saturn come together almost every 60 years, after Jupiter has made five revolutions and Saturn two revolutions of the Sun. Two "years" of Saturn is 58.9 Earth years, just short of 60. The number 60 is also almost exactly five Jupiter revolutions (59.31 years to be precise). The Russian scientist Immanuel Velikovsky believed that at some time in the past Jupiter may have lost some of its mass, so it is just possible that five ancient Jupiterian "years" might at one time have been exactly 60 Earth years.

The number 60 formed the basis of many ancient counting systems, in much the same way as we use the number ten today. This is still evident in France where numbers are counted up to 60, "soixante", after which 60 forms the stem to which the additions are added, so 70, for example, is expressed as "60 plus 10". Sixty is also the magic number used by Chinese astrologers to denote a completed cycle.

Copernicus proved that Saturn and Jupiter revolved around the Sun

The Code of Nostradamus

Nostradamus used a planetary "clock" of approximately 60 years to date his prophecies. In a letter to King Henri II of France, he identified 1606 as a key prediction year.

If we add 60 years to 1606, taking our clue from *Liber Vaticinationem*, we arrive at 1666, the year of one of Nostradamus's very few precisely dated prophecies (II:51), the Fire of London, and, incidentally, a highly significant millennial year, being 1000 plus the number of the Beast of the Apocalypse of St John. A further 60 years added to 1666 brings us to 1726. In Century III, quatrain 77 (III:77) Nostradamus gives another date:

"The third climate included under Aries;
In the year 1727 in October:
The King of Persia will be captured by those of Egypt:
Battle, death, loss: a great shame to the cross."

This quatrain is amazingly correct: it contains not only the year but also the month and the place of the event. In October 1727 a peace was concluded between the Turks (symbolized here by Egypt) and the Persians.

Quatrain 77 is a milestone among the reams of undated predictions included in the majority of the prophet's quatrains. In it we also find confirmation of his 60-year planetary clock, for the first line refers to the "third climate under Aries", and this is the third period of 60 years. Also, if it

The Great Fire of London was part of Nostradamus's 60-year cycles for dating the future

is "under Aries", it is ruled by Aries, the first sign of the zodiac.

From 1727 we add another 60 years to reach 1787, the year in which the parliament of Paris demanded the summoning of the States-General. King Louis XVI prevaricated, but the States-General met at Versailles two years later. The Paris mob stormed the Bastille, and in 1792 the royal family of France was imprisoned and the French Republic was established.

This exact date, 1792, is specifically mentioned by Nostradamus in his letter to Henri II, where he says that the French people "will think it to be a renovation of time". In that year the French revolutionary calendar came into force, an amazing foresight by Nostradamus. For Nostradamus, a staunch royalist, these visions of the French Revolution must have been profoundly disturbing.

From our key date of 1727 until the end of the world – AD 3797 according to Nostradamus – is 2070 years, almost exactly 70 revolutions of Jupiter. This is further confirmation that Nostradamus used this orbital period of Jupiter as a building block for his astronomical calculations which gave the dates to his prophecies, which dates until now have eluded interpreters for almost 450 years.

Nostradamus left certain significant dates in his prophecies as both a guide to dating the others and as a more than adequate proof that he was able to pinpoint very significant events down to the year and even to the month. This method can be applied to the dating of the arrival of the Third Antichrist, the wars of this period and the final Apocalypse.

GEOGRAPHICAL PRECISION OF THE PROPHET

In his letter to Henri II, Nostradamus professes to make prophetic calculations concerning "towns and cities, throughout Europe, Africa, and a part of Asia". In actuality, some 60 per cent of the prophet's predictions pertained to Europe, and predominantly his home country, France (28 per cent of the quatrains solely concern France). Only 3 per cent of the quatrains concern Muslim North Africa, parts of central Asia and the Middle East, with the balance having no perceivable geographic location and therefore likely to do with events in France as well.

There have been many claims for mentions of America in the prophecies. "Americh" is directly referred to in only one quatrain (X:66). The context, though, is totally British, with explicit references to London and Scotland. Even the numbering of this quatrain, 1066, is a numeric reference to Britain. Attempts to interpret his prophecies in relation to North or South America, Australia, non-Muslim Africa or Southeast Asia are at best speculative, at worst just plain wrong.

King Henri II was given the key

The storming of the Bastille – the French Revolution was a turning point

The Monarchy under Threat?

The British monarchy has had more than its fair share of trouble in the last decade of the millennium.

A major blow was dealt to the British royal family when a large section of Windsor Castle, the Queen's family home, burnt down, with the fire service apparently unable to contain the blaze. The Castle was uninsured, and repairs have been estimated at some £60 million ($89 million).

This personal sadness was compounded by constitutional strife arising in a former colony, Australia. The Prime Minister of Australia, Paul Keating, is pushing to turn Australia into a republic, cutting the old colonial ties that bind the country to the UK and removing the Queen as the notional head of state.

Finally, and perhaps most traumatically, the monarchy has been torn apart by talk of possible divorce of two of the Queen's sons, Prince Andrew and the heir apparent, Prince Charles.

In quatrain VI:59 Nostradamus seems to have given some advance warning of the drama played out between Prince Andrew and his wife,

Sarah, Duchess of York

Lady Sarah Ferguson, which hit the headlines in 1991 and 1992:
"The lady, furious in an adulterous rage,
Will conspire against her Prince, but not speak to him.
But the culprit will soon be known,
So that seventeen will be martyred."

Lady Sarah Ferguson was so upset by newspaper reports of her alleged adultery with Texan businessman Steve Wyatt that she went on a trip to Indonesia without Prince Andrew and without speaking to him first. The newspapers published photographs of the Princess with Mr Wyatt, who is obviously the culprit mentioned in the quatrain. The identities of the 17 who will suffer "martydom" because of their actions have yet to be revealed.

Also in 1991, a rift between Princess Diana and Prince Charles became

Windsor Castle, seat and symbol of British monarchy, goes up in flames

public knowledge. Several newspapers carried reports of an alleged telephone conversation between the Princess and a close friend, James Gilbey. A book detailing the Princess's miserable marriage and rejection by Prince Charles stoked the fires of speculation still further. These events may well be reflected in quatrain VI:74:

"She who was cast out will return to reign,
Her enemies found among conspirators.
More than ever will her reign be triumphant.
At three and seventy death is very sure."

This suggests that in the end the popularity of the Princess will guarantee her a welcome return to the centre of monarchy, with her perhaps living until the age of 73.

Another quatrain (VII:83) may well refer to the same events:

"Wind warm, counsels, tears, timidity
By night in bed assailed without arms:
Great calamity from oppression,
The wedding song converted, weeping and tears."

The initial reluctance by the royal family to air the matter with the press is put down to timidity here. The second line refers to the by now infamous slanging matches between the Prince and Princess, peppered with accusations. Princess Diana felt very oppressed by both Charles and the harassment of the press during the execution of her public duties.

What does Nostradamus say of the outcome of these events? An alternative quatrain which appears only in some of the early editions, VIII:2, may provide the answer:

"Several will come, and will speak of peace,

Charles and Diana – will "she who was cast out" return to reign?

Between Monarchs and very powerful lords:
But it will not be accorded so soon,
Unless they become more obedient than the other."

This quatrain implies that the royal family must bow, at least publicly, to the demands of their advisors.

THE OUTCOME

The quatrain which seems to sum up the eventual outcome is quatrain X:40:

"The young heir to the British realm,
Whom his dying father will have recommended:
The latter dead, 'Lonole' [London?] will dispute with him,
And from the son the realm demanded"

This quatrain is often interpreted as carrying a prediction of the abdication of Edward VIII in 1936. It might, however, fit better with the present circumstances of the British monarchy. One reading might be that Prince Charles, "the young heir to the British realm" is recommended by his father Prince Philip to take the throne. As the father in the quatrain is dying, these events are obviously some way off. It is unclear who Lonole is, but as it is printed in the original French in capitals, it is likely to be some kind of anagram or pun, but it may equally well be a reference to London or Parliament.

Finally, in the last line, Parliament demands the realm back, perhaps even requesting Charles to abdicate. In order to resolve the question, the government may be forced to put the question of a republic to a referendum. The last line is not clear as to whether a republic is the outcome or if it is simply a request to Charles to abdicate. After all, Charles has been a fairly unlucky name for British kings.

The Third Antichrist

Interpreters of the prophecies of Nostradamus have identified Napoleon as the First Antichrist and Hitler as the Second. Who is the Third?

Nostradamus mentions the Third Antichrist in his letter to Henri II of France, dated 27 June 1558. This being will appear after the Germans have been "driven back by the whole of the Latin race". The timing and circumstances of his coming are open to conjecture. The terminology suggests war, but it could equally indicate some internal adjustment in the European Community. In the same letter, Nostradamus says more about the timing of the arrival of the Antichrist:
"Then the great Empire of the Antichrist will begin where once was Attila's empire, the new Xerxes will descend with great and countless numbers."

Attila (c. 406–53), King of the Huns, nicknamed "the Scourge of God", claimed divine descent and the rulership of the world. Nostradamus sees the Antichrist in similar terms, as a figure claiming to rule the world and beginning his rise to power from Germany. He also refers to the Antichrist as a new Xerxes. Xerxes

(485–65 BC), King of Persia, wanted to conquer Greece, and burnt Athens to the ground. This passage suggests that the Antichrist will want to destroy the foundations of Western democracy, symbolized by Athens.

Nostradamus gives physical signs of the Antichrist's arrival:
"This will be preceded by an eclipse of the sun, more obscure and tenebrose than has ever been since the creation of the world, except that [eclipse] after the death and passion of Jesus Christ."

The three next total eclipses of the sun visible in the UK and Europe will be on 11 August 1999, 23 September 2090 and 7 October 2135. One will mark the arrival of the Antichrist. The last coincides with Max Toth's supposed fourth incarnation of the Messiah, but in quatrain X:72 Nostradamus refers to the first of these dates. It is one of only 17 specific year identifications given by the prophet:
"In the year 1999, and seven months, From the sky will come the great King of Terror.

Attila, the Scourge of God

He will bring to life the great King of the Mongols. Before and after war reigns happily."

If you ignore the adjustment to the calendar that occurred after Nostradamus's death (the change from the Julian to the Gregorian calendar, in 1582), this eclipse will occur at the end of the seventh month of 1999.

The contemporary American psychic Jeane Dixon had a vision of the birth of the Antichrist on 5 February 1962, the day of another solar eclipse. If we accept this as truth, then he will come to power at the age of 37, also on a solar eclipse.

Nostradamus gives us one more time clue. Just before the time of the Antichrist there will be found someone "from the 50th degree [of latitude], who will renovate the whole Christian Church". As the 50th parallel of latitude goes almost exactly through Cracow in Poland, it might be that Nostradamus was referring to the only

Pope to have come from that city, John Paul II. His papacy will precede the reign of the Antichrist, further confirming 1999 as the correct date.

Who will deliver the world from the Third Antichrist? Nostradamus writes "the coming of the Holy Ghost, proceeding from the 48th degree [of latitude], will make a transmigration, chasing away the abomination of the Antichrist, who will have made war upon the royal person of the Pope and upon the Christian Church".

The saviour who will dethrone the Antichrist will come from the 48th degree of latitude, which suggests Le Mans, Orleans, or possibly Vienna.

Elsewhere (VIII:77) Nostradamus suggests that the Antichrist will survive for 27 years:

"The Third Antichrist very soon annihilated,
Seven and twenty years of blood will his war last:
The heretics dead, captives exiled,
Blood human body water reddened on land to hail."

After many wars and much destruction, there will "be almost renewed another reign of Saturn, a golden age". Saturn must not be confused with Satan. Nostradamus, as we know, measures time in accordance with the cycles of the planets Saturn and Jupiter, and regards Saturn in a classical Greek way, as the ruler of a departed golden age. So we return to this golden age after 25 years of misrule by the Third Antichrist, which brings the date to 2024, close to Woldben's calculation of the birth date of the Age of Aquarius (2023) and Alice Bailey's "manifestation of the Fourth Ray" in 2025.

THE SECOND ANTICHRIST IN THE 20TH CENTURY

Mixed in with the prophecy of the Third Antichrist are passages which plainly relate to Hitler, the Second Antichrist, the 20th century, Communism and Fascism. The passages are confused because both the Second and Third Antichrist arise in Germany. Nostradamus mentions the rise of Hitler, the Second Antichrist, in his famous letter to Henri II: ". . . the all-powerful land between the rivers of Europe, to 45, and others to 41, 42, and 47. And in that time and those countries the infernal power will set . . . against the Church of Jesus Christ. This will constitute the Second Antichrist."

The reference "to 45" identifies the terminating year as 1945, and hence we must conclude that the Second Antichrist was Adolf Hitler. Nostradamus is aware that "the said reign of Antichrist will last only to the death of him [Hitler] who was born near the [commencement] of the century." Hitler was, in fact, born in 1889.

This passage is preceded by a strange sentence: "all this accompanied with the procreation of the New Babylon, a miserable prostitute big with the abomination of the first holocaust". The word "holocaust" is applied to Hitler's attempt to exterminate the Jews, so this sentence ties in one of the greatest atrocities of the Second Antichrist with the Whore of Babylon who will be associated with the sins to be committed by the Third Antichrist.

Adolf Hitler, the Second Antichrist, inflames his followers

Islamic Expansionism

In recent years some of Europe's economic strength has passed to the oil-rich states of the Middle East.

Protesting Libyans in Tripoli assert the strength of Islamic fundamentalism

Not since the Crusades of the Middle Ages, which hoped to "recover" the Holy Land of Palestine for Christianity, has the West's interest in the Middle East been so strong. The predictions for the fate of the region made by Nostradamus have been amazingly detailed (see panel).

The interest of Christian countries in the Muslim world has often been associated with the millennium. For example, the return of the Jews to their spiritual homeland was assisted by many Christians because they believed that such a resettlement was a necessary precondition for the Second Coming of Christ. This was finally achieved in 1947 with the establishment of the state of Israel, just half a century before the millennium. The consequence has been to provoke much Arab opposition.

In quatrain VI:80 Nostradamus predicted two Islamic expansionist invasions for the late 1990s, one from Morocco (represented by the city of Fez), the other from Iran (Persia).
"From Fez the [Islamic] kingdom will stretch out to Europe,
The city blazes, and the sword will slash:
The great man of Asia with a great troop by land and sea,
So that the blues, Persians, the cross to death is driven."

Nostradamus had a great deal to say about the Turks and the Arabs, who in his day threatened to surround Europe in a pincer movement. Muslim lords had attacked Spain, reaching as far as the Pyrenees, while the Turks had invaded Eastern Europe as far as the walls of Vienna. In quatrain VI:80, however, it is the Iranians (Persians) who pose the threat.

A leader from Asia is also involved, and the attack will result in the burning of a city and many deaths "by the sword". The reference may be to a holy war, or jihad, with Muslim armies converging from North Africa and from Iran against Christian Europe, just like the Muslim invasion of Spain 700 years ago. However, it is more likely to be one last outburst of Islamic fundamentalism of the sort for which Colonel Gaddafi of Libya has become famous.

One line from another quatrain (I:73) seems to imply that the Iranians will incite the Tunisians, Algerians and the Moroccans to join in this action:
"Tunisia, Algeria stirred up by Persians."

In this quatrain the French are blamed for their negligence which has allowed the unrest to boil over. Nostradamus seems to be quite aware of France's colonial involvement in North Africa, although this would happen years after his death. In quatrain I:18 the finger is again pointed at the French:

"*Because of the Gallic [French] discord and negligence
A passage will be opened to Mohammed:
The land and sea of Siena soaked in blood,
Marseilles covered with sails and ships*"

The passage "opened to Moham-med" might simply mean the relaxing of French immigration controls against Muslim immigrants. Siena is an un-certain translation of "Senoise" which might instead refer to immigrants from a war-torn Senegal, a former French colony on the west coast of Africa. Marseilles is obviously the French port of entry from North Africa.

Quatrain V:55 contains a suggestion that a great Islamic conqueror will be born in "Arabia Felix", the south-eastern portion of Arabia that is now known as the Yemen. So far this region has had little to do with Western poli-tics, being allied with first Saudi Arabia and later Egypt:

"*In the country of Arabia Felix
There will be born one powerful in the law of Mohammed:
To vex Spain, to conquer Grenada,
And move by sea against the Ligurian people*"

The Ligurians are the people of Genoa in Italy, while Grenada (properly Granada) is in Spain. This new Muslim ruler will in some sense reconquer the southern part of Spain for Islam. He will also move by sea against Genoa.

Further Islamic incursions do seem to be in store for Europe (see panel).

SADDAM HUSSEIN AND THE WHORE OF BABYLON

The most recent war in the Middle East, instigated by the Iraqi leader Saddam Hussein in 1991, was clearly predicted by Nostradamus. The prophet described it in amazing detail in quatrain VIII:70:

"*He will enter, wicked, unpleasant, infamous
Tyrannizing over Mesopotamia.
All friends made by the adulterous woman.
The land dreadful and black of aspect.*"

Saddam Hussein certainly entered Kuwait in a wicked and underhand manner. He is still tyrannizing Mesopotamia, the ancient Greek name for Iraq. The "adulterous woman" might be a 20th-century friend and ally of Hussein, but it is more likely to be a reference to the Biblical Whore of Babylon predicted in the Apocalypse of St John. Babylon's position as capital of the region has been taken over by Baghdad, Saddam Hussein's capital, but it is still from this region that many people expect to see fulfilment of Biblical prophecies.

The last line is a perfect descrip-tion of the huge black clouds that hung over Kuwait after Saddam Hussein deliberately set fire to that nation's oil wells, thus creating a major ecological headache.

Oilfields in Kuwait, "the land dreadful and black of aspect", blaze out of control

The Fall of the Vatican

The end of the long line of popes has already been clearly prophesied by St Malachy, but it remains for Nostradamus to tell us how this will come about.

Should these cardinals in Synod fear persecution by the Kings of "Aquilon"?

In his famous letter to Henri II of France, dated 27 June 1558, Nostradamus states (in paragraph 50) that "the persecution of the Ecclesiastical folk [priests] will have its origin in the power of the Kings of 'Aquilon'" [the North]. He continues, "great Vicar of the Cope [the Pope] shall be put back to his pristine state; but, desolated and abandoned by all, will return to the sanctuary destroyed by Paganism, when the Old and New Testament will be thrust out and burnt. After that Antichrist will be the infernal prince. Then at this last epoch, all the kingdoms of Christianity, as well as the infidel world, will be shaken during the space of twenty-five years." After the binding of Satan, "then shall commence between God and man a universal peace. There he shall abide for the space of a thousand years".

In quatrain X:70 he announces the death of a Pope in a way which has not yet occurred, suggesting that this must be a reference to one of the three remaining popes.
"Through an object the eye will swell very much,
Burning so much that the snow will fall:
The fields watered will come to shrink,
As the primate succumbs at Reggio"

No pope has yet died at Reggio in Italy, so one must deduce that this is yet to come. The death seems to be linked to an eye infection, so painful that "the snows will fall", a phrase which perhaps means that blindness or cataract will affect the pope's eye.

In one quatrain (V:15) Nostradamus predicts that the Pope will be taken captive:
"The great Pontiff taken captive while navigating,
The great one thereafter to fail the clergy in tumult
Second one elected absent his estate declines,
His favourite bastard to death broken on the wheel"

This is a very daring prophecy which does not yet seem to have taken place. The only popes to be taken captive since 1555 are Pius VI and Pius VII, both captured by Napoleon at Fontainbleau before 1814. Quatrain V:15 has sometimes been associated with these two events. However, the passage may indicate that the Third Antichrist will take control of the papacy rather than actually physically imprison the pope himself.

The capture of the pope during a sea voyage is a possible interpretation of the first line. The second line suggests that the pope deserts or fails his priests, perhaps by fleeing Rome. Line three may refer to his frightened successor hiding, or merely suggest that as the pope has fled from Rome his "estate", the papacy, will decline.

The last line is more appropriate to a medieval pope; the last pope famous for his bastards was Paul III (1534–49). The last line has a similarly medieval ring to it. The wheel is no longer used as an instrument of torture, so perhaps the reference should be interpreted in a

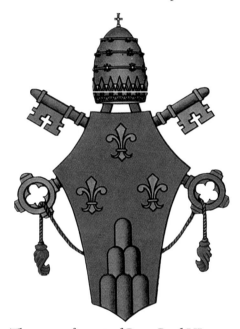

The coat-of-arms of Pope Paul VI

modern sense; for example, a car wheel, involved in a traffic accident.

An interesting connection concerning the impending schism (see panel) is thrown up by quatrain V:46:

"Quarrels and new schemes by the red hats
When the Sabine will have been elected:
They will produce great sophisms against him,
And Rome will be injured by those of Alba"

The "red hats" is a reference to cardinals. A cardinal from the Sabine country (northwest of Rome) will be elected pope. However, one faction of cardinals will scheme against him and refuse to acknowledge his election.

The last line suggests that Rome itself rather than the Vatican will be attacked, but the identity of the "Albanois" is difficult to decipher. Some commentators have suggested that this is a reference to Albanians. A more likely explanation is that they are a faction whose flag or symbol is white: "albus" means white. More plausible still is to read Albanois as a reference to the Albenses, the original Latin people. If this interpretation is accepted, Nostradamus is suggesting an attack from within, strengthening the idea of schism in the Church.

Whichever interpretation is taken, it seems that the Vatican will experience considerable trouble within the reigns of the next three popes (including the present one) and that the institution itself may well come under the control of Nostradamus's Third Antichrist.

THE BRITISH CONNECTION

Quatrain VI:22 suggests an interesting connection between Britain and the papacy:
"Within the land of the great heavenly temple,
Nephew murdered at London through feigned peace:
The barque will then become schismatic,
Sham liberty will be proclaimed everywhere"

This quatrain continues the use of the word barque as a metaphor for the papacy. The "land of the great heavenly temple" would seem to be England. The murder in London of the nephew of a ruler may already have happened, but there is reason to believe that it has not, because the other coinciding factor – doctrinal schism in the Roman Church – has not been present. The Church of England has recently experienced a schism of sorts over its decision to allow women to become priests, with some conservative members of the clergy threatening to quit. Nostradamus is quite specific, however, and his reference to the barque of St Peter means the Roman Catholic Church and no other.

The last line might refer to false freedoms that will be proclaimed by the Third Antichrist.

Women priests have created a schism

The Seven Millenniums

According to Nostradamus the Earth was created in 4137 BC, which is not far off Bishop Ussher's date of 4004 BC. We are at present living at the end of the sixth millennium.

Hecate, the goddess of witchcraft

Nostradamus's vision of what the seventh millennium holds is bleak indeed, especially for the Christian Churches. He depicted the seventh millennium as "the time when the adversaries of Jesus Christ and of His Church shall begin to multiply in great force".

The commencement of the seventh millennium is now almost upon us. Quatrain X:72 announces war unequivocally in 1999:

*"The year 1999, seventh month,
From the sky will come a great King of Terror:
To bring back to life the great King of the Mongols,
Before and after Mars reigns"*

Such a gloomy prediction seems appropriate for the period immediately preceding the millennium. The seventh month will be September, because Nostradamus counted the beginning of the year from 1 March. The reign of

Mars is symbolic of war. The King of Terror is most likely to be the Antichrist, although it is possible that it is some horrendous weapon.

The next quatrain speaks of the Last Judgement, with pagan overtones:
*"The present time together with the past
Will be judged by the great Jovialist:
The world too late will be tired of him,
And through the clergy oath-taker
[will be] disloyal"*

The first line suggests a judgement of the living as well as the dead. The judge is either "great Jove" himself, father of the Roman gods, or more likely the pagan leader, the Antichrist. Too late the world will discover who he is and tire of his rule. That the Jovian figure is the Antichrist is bolstered by the clergy disloyally taking an oath to him, rather than remaining firm in their faith.

The next quatrain (X:74), also dated, refers to further developments in the same period:

Will the Olympic Games of AD 2000 see a great pagan sacrifice and revival?

"The year of the great seventh number accomplished,
It will appear at the time of the games of the Hecatomb:
Not far from the great millennial age, When the buried will go out from their tombs"

The "year of the great seventh number" refers to the arrival of the seventh millennium, in AD 2000. Hecatomb means sacrifice, of 100 oxen in the time of the ancient Olympic Games. The word "hecatomb" also suggests Hecate, the goddess of night, magic and enchantment. Nostradamus confirms in this quatrain and in his letter to Henri II of France that, after the binding of Satan, "then shall commence between God and man a universal peace. There he shall abide for the space of a thousand years."

Although apocalyptic events will occur at the end of the century, according to Nostradamus the Earth will survive until AD 3797. He states "near the seventh millenary . . . the world [will be] approaching its great conflagration, although by my . . . prophecies, the course of time runs much further on".

Nostradamus also predicts a change in climate at this time when "the rains will be so diminished and such abundance of fire and fiery missiles shall fall from the heavens that nothing shall escape the holocaust. This will occur before the last conflagration".

In a letter to his son César, Nostradamus foretells the very last days as "the worldwide conflagration which is to bring so many catastrophes and such revolutions that scarcely any lands will not be covered by water, and this will last until all has perished save history and geography themselves."

HOW OLD IS THE WORLD?

Did God create Adam in 4758 BC, as Nostradamus claimed?

In order to determine the end of the world we need to know the date of its beginning. Nostradamus appears to have computed the date in two different ways in the same document, his letter to King Henri II. In the tenth paragraph Nostradamus calculates the time which elapsed between the creation of Adam and the birth of Christ as 1242+1080+515 (or 516) +570+1350 = 4757 or 4758 years. This gives AD 2242 as the end of the seventh millennium, and the time of the Apocalypse.

Later in the same letter (paragraphs 39–40), however, he comes up with a different calculation, plainly telling us that this will not agree with the previous chronology. From Adam to Christ appears now to be 1506+600+1+295+100+60+130+430+480+490 = 4092 years and 2 months. For some strange reason, possibly due to a missing sentence, Nostradamus totals these numbers as 4173 years and 8 months. It is not credible that anyone as skilful as Nostradamus in astrology could accidentally make such a basic arithmetical error.

Traditional Christian wisdom, as stated by Archishop James Ussher, has it that the world was created in 4004 BC. This means that the seventh millennium begins in January 1997. In the light of quatrain X:72, however, the year is more likely to be AD 2000.

The total lifespan of the world from 4173 BC to 3797 AD works out at 7970 years, ignoring the months. If we calculate it from 4758 BC we arrive at 8555 years. The former figure seems to be the more significant, as it is 30 years short of exactly 8 millennia.

KINGDOM
of the
CULTS

*Many Christian cults spawned their own
messiahs. Many disciples followed them
only too willingly, from the women of the
Abode of Love who buried their dead
standing up, through cults with millions of
followers and powerful publishing empires,
to the flaming Apocalypse of Waco and the
strange female messiah of modern Russia.*

Prophecies on Plates of Gold

There is probably no American religious group which has had a more colourful or fascinating history than the Mormons, who were founded in the 19th century by the New England prophet Joseph Smith.

Joseph Smith

Vermont-born Smith received his first revelation in spring 1820, when he was only 14. He was praying in the woods near his home when two figures suddenly appeared. One pointed to the other and said, "This is my beloved Son, hear Him!" Smith immediately assumed he was experiencing a visitation from God himself and lost no time in asking which was the correct sect or church for him to join in order to be saved. The figure replied that "all their creeds [were] an abomination".

His second vision occurred two years later when an angel, or "messenger from God", as he put it, visited his bedside and told him that he had work to do in spreading the true gospel.

From that moment on Smith had a burning compulsion to bring the real truth, whatever that might be, to his fellow men. This angel, Moroni, told Smith that a book written on golden plates, giving an account of the former inhabitants of North America and containing the "fullness of the everlasting Gospel" as delivered by the Saviour to the ancient inhabitants of North America, had been deposited on the hillside outside the town where Smith lived. With the plates were the Urim and Thummim, the two stones which were the prophetic oracle and interpreter of God's words and worn by the ancient Jewish High Priests.

As you can imagine, the next day Smith went straight to the location on Cumorah Hill indicated by the angel, where he promptly found the book of golden plates deposited in a stone box with the stones Urim and Thummim, and the High Priest's breastplate. The angel, who paid him a visit on the hill, too, told Smith not to take out the contents of the stone box, but to return to the same location every year for the next four years. Finally, on 22

Joseph Smith receives the golden plates from the angel Moroni

The Mormon leader Brigham Young

September 1827, at the autumn Equinox, the angel entrusted the plates and other paraphernalia to Smith.

Smith married Emma Hale and moved in with her father, where he began the task of translating the text written on the golden plates. The text was not written in Hebrew or even Greek as one might have imagined, but in "Reformed Egyptian". To satisfy Martin Harris, a potential financier and publisher of the book, Smith provided examples of this unique language together with his translation of it. The financier took them to a Professor Charles Anthon who identified the characters as a mixture of "Egyptian, Chaldean, Assyriac and Arabic". How anyone untutored could translate such an esoteric mixture is hard to say, but apparently divine inspiration triumphed over mere book learning, and the translation progressed.

In 1929, Smith and a friend, Oliver Cowdery, met another heavenly messenger while praying in the woods. This messenger, who identified himself

THE PRIESTHOOD OF MELCHIZEDEK

The original Melchizedek was called "Priest of the Most High God". He was a Caananite priest and possibly king of Jerusalem at the time of Abraham. By one sect of Gnostics (these were early Christians who claimed to have certain mystical knowledge denied to other people) he was held to be an earlier incarnation of Christ. This strange view, that God has reincarnated more than once, is supported in the Epistle of Paul to the Hebrews 7:3 where Melchizedek is referred to as "like unto the Son of God". In the same chapter St Paul even questions Christ's ancestry by suggesting that the tribe of Judah, from which Christ descended, was not renowned for producing great priests or prophets, as was the tribe of Levi or the descendants of Melchizedek.

All male Mormons of a certain age, good standing and good character may be received into one or other of these two priesthoods, Levi or Melchizedek. It is for this reason that the Mormons have a very large male priesthood and a predominantly female laity.

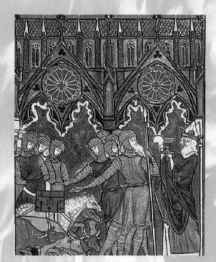

Melchizedek, like the son of God

as John the Baptist, immediately initiated both Smith and Oliver into "the priesthood of Aaron". Aaron was the elder brother of Moses and the first in the long line of Jewish High Priests to come after the Israelites' escape from captivity in Egypt. It is unclear how John the Baptist was able to confer the Jewish priesthood upon these two, but according to Smith he did, and later the pair received an even higher accolade, that of the priesthood of Melchizedek (see panel).

Smith's translation of the book of the golden leaves was published on 26 March 1830, close to the spring Equinox, two and a half years after he had begun working on it. A few days later the "Church of Jesus Christ of Latter-day Saints", as the Mormons refer to their church, was officially constituted at Fayette in New York.

The Mormons eventually settled at Nauvoo. Here, Joseph Smith and his brother were killed when an anti-Mormon mob stormed the jail where they were being held for destroying a printworks. Brigham Young (1801–77), who succeeded the martyred Smith, moved the colony westwards to Salt Lake City, Utah, which is still the headquarters and home of the sect.

Baptism for 80 Million Dead

"Celestial marriage" and "baptism for the dead" are among the ceremonies celebrated in Mormon temples. Ironically, their programme of "baptism for the dead" has resulted in the mass forced baptism of the faithful of other churches.

London Mormon Temple – baptism for thousands, both living and dead

Mormons believe in the literal gathering of the Ten Tribes of Israel in America, before the return of Christ who will then reign over them personally. This will happen close to the millennium in three distinct stages:

1. The Gathering of Ephraim. The tribe of Ephraim from whom Joseph Smith claimed (presumably spiritual) descent is to gather first in Zion, the site of the New Jerusalem. The site of Zion was previously thought to be the city of Independence, Missouri, but is now designated as a site near the Rocky Mountains. This gathering is progressing at the moment.

2. The Gathering of the Jews. This gathering of the descendants of the Kingdom of Judah (not the descendants of the Kingdom of Israel) is currently taking place in Palestine, as also predicted by the Old Testament prophets. This prediction just recently got a boost from the signing of the PLO/Israeli peace accord in September 1993. The Temple, and possibly the city, of Jerusalem have yet to be rebuilt before the return of Christ.

3. The Gathering of the Ten Lost Tribes. Distinct from the previous gathering, there will be a gathering of the ten lost tribes of Israel, which are still hiding somewhere "in the lands of the north". They are to regroup and go to Zion where they will be received by the Ephraimites who have already arrived there. This has not yet happened, and may well be quite tricky to arrange, unless you believe the British Israelite doctrine that these lost tribes are, in fact, the British!

The Mormons believe that when these three gatherings are complete, Christ will return to earth. For them, the Millennium constitutes a period of 1000 years beginning at about the year AD 2000. There will be two resurrections, one at the beginning and one at the end of this millennial period. In the first resurrection the believing dead will be raised, and in rapture will literally rise through the air to meet the descending Christ, touching down again with him as he lands. Charitably, the Mormons include the "good heathen" in this resurrection. The wicked, on the other hand, will be "burned as stubble" without a second chance, and during the millennium their spirits will remain in some gigantic spirit prison.

Shortly after the beginning of the millennium, in the year AD 2000, the "City of Enoch" (or the New Jerusalem) will descend from heaven

Preparing for the millennium

and materialize in the prepared site of Zion. Satan will be bound and his power to do evil severely limited. People living during this time will die if they are unrepentant, or alternatively become immortal at the age of 100 instead of facing death, an attractive prospect. After his return to Earth, Christ will rule in the flesh over two capital cities, Jerusalem in Palestine and "Zion" in the USA. After this the Earth will rest from wars for a further 1000 beatific years.

At the end of the millennial period in AD 3000 there will be a second round of resurrections, Satan will be released, and the very small number of those who follow him will become the "Sons of Perdition". These unfortunates are destined never to be redeemed, and to eternally reside in Hell. With his new converts, Satan will again attempt, albeit unsuccessfully, to storm heaven. After his defeat the Earth shall become "celestialized" and a fit home for the remaining spiritualized humans, who will receive varying degrees of immortality.

80 MILLION DEAD HELD IN COMPUTERS

The Mormon crusade to "baptize the dead" has resulted in the sect accumulating vast quantities of genealogical information, including birth, baptism and marriage details, for over 80,000,000 dead people!

This data is stored in memory banks in Salt Lake City. Copies are kept in enormous tunnels bored into the mountains, in what must be one of the safest data storage facilities in the world today. It is a comforting thought that if the world were wiped out by some apocalyptic cataclysm, the details of all these people would be available for inspection at some remote time in the future.

The more than 80 million dead so documented are not necessarily Mormons, but are mostly of Anglo-Saxon descent, and seldom aware that their details are being added to and preserved by a sect they may never have heard of.

There are several non-religious by-products of this extraordinary endeavour. First, the records, once computerized, are supplied on microfiche cards at Mormon centres throughout the world, and are used extensively by ordinary genealogists and family historians.

Recently researchers into "genetic epidemiology" – research into the incidence, distribution and control or dissemination of a disease in the overall population – have been using this vast collection of records to trace back diseases to the parents, grandparents and great-grandparents of current patients. This enables researchers to then contact other branches of a family to trace genes which predispose to certain conditions. Maybe medical help will come to some of these potential patients, instead of the religious salvation originally intended.

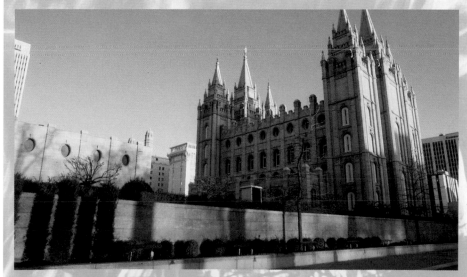

The imposing Mormon Temple at Salt Lake City, Utah

Jehovah's Witnesses

Russell predicted millennial events

Charles Taze Russell (1852–1916), the founding father of the Jehovah's Witnesses, calculated a date for the end of the world, Armageddon and the Second Coming of Christ. The year 1999 is the current expectation.

Russell first put forward 1874 as the date of the establishment of the Kingdom of God, and when this failed he settled upon 1 October 1914. He must have been one of the few people to be pleased by the start of World War I in the summer of that year. When Christ failed to materialize after this promising start, Russell said He was invisible, in fact merely a heavenly transaction in rulership. Armageddon was then comfortably predicted for 61 years later, in 1975, a date subsequently revised several times.

Armageddon will be Jehovah's decisive (though not final) battle against his enemies. The Witnesses regard this as a necessary battle to unseat Satan, the previous ruler of the world, before the ushering in of a glorious new world. The price will be high: over two billion dead, none of whom will be raised up to Heaven. One side will use bows, arrows, handstaves and spears, and the other cloudbursts, floods, earthquakes, hailstones, all-consuming fires and flesh-eating plagues. At the end of the

battle Christ will cast Satan and his demonic associates into the abyss.

Cleansed by Armageddon, the Earth will become a temperate garden, an earthly paradise, replacing the paradise lost at the dawn of history. Beasts will be at peace one with another and man will have dominion over the "lower animals". The millennium will literally be a thousand-year period reigned over by Christ, with no ageing, no disease, no crime, no vice and no death. The earth will be populated by the survivors of Armageddon.

Russell arrived at these dates by plucking from the Bible whichever passages suited his purpose, regardless of context. This technique is still used by members of the movement today. From that old stalwart of all interpreters, the Book of Daniel, chapter 7:14, Russell deduced that Christ was to be given a kingdom which would never be destroyed, by God, "the Ancient of days".

Christ was supposed to receive this kingdom at the end of the "appointed times of the nations", calculated at 2520 days (see panel), for which read years. Prophets were often said to use "days" as a sort of shorthand for years, a practice supposedly supported in Ezekiel 4:6: "I have appointed thee each day for a year". To arrive at a date for the millennial year, you add 2520 to 607 (BC), when Israel lost its sovereignty and came under the rule of the armies of Babylon.

The Witnesses' HQ in New York

But to return to the beginnings of the Jehovah's Witnesses; in 1879 Russell first published a magazine called *Zion's Watch Tower and Herald of Christ's Presence*, which helped to publicize the new movement. Five years later Russell's society was legally incorporated.

The millennial bent of the organization was apparent from the beginning. In a series of books called "Millennial Dawn" Russell tantalized his disciples with promises of the kingdom near at hand. Over six million copies of the first book found homes.

In 1912 Russell began work on one of his most ambitious projects, the Photo-Drama of Creation. Through a mixture of slides and motion pictures with sound, years ahead of its time, Russell portrayed events from the Creation to the end of Christ's supposed 1000-year reign. Up to 35,000 people daily were seeing Russell's show when it opened in 1914. Just as the Jehovah's Witnesses had discovered the power of the printing presses, so they recognized the importance of cinema as a medium for spreading news of their cause.

Russell survived his 1914 prophecy by only two years. After his death the leadership of the organization was disputed, and further trouble followed in 1918 when the Canadian government forbade anyone to possess copies of the *Watchtower*. Also in 1918, eight leading members were found guilty of refusing to serve in the US military, an offence for which their leader was sentenced to 20 years' imprisonment, although a year later all the men were freed.

To get round this problem, which arose again during the Second World War, a number of members became 'ministers' full time, which helped to expand the movement.

The Church is now a huge organization with its own printing presses and sophisticated administration infrastructure. In New York alone, the Witnesses run seven factories and a large office complex.

The Jehovah's Witnesses deny any conscious existence after death. Man, according to them, will remain in the grave until the millennium, when the favoured few will be resurrected in a spiritual body. There are more than 3,750,00 Jehovah's Witnesses in the world today, but according to their own scriptures there is only room for 144,000 souls to reign as the elect with Christ in Heaven.

CALCULATING THE DATE OF CHRIST'S RETURN

The starting point for the Jehovah's Witnesses is, as we have seen, 607 BC, the date the people of Israel were subjugated by Babylon. Nebuchadnezzar is told in Daniel 4:23 that he shall be reduced to the state of a beast of the field, "till seven times pass over him".

This is construed as seven years or seven times 360 (the number of days in a year, according to the usage then assumed current), which equals 2520.

This last figure is interpreted as 2520 years, using the year for a day rule, which is then added to 607 BC. We then get the year AD 1914 as the date Christ was due to return to rule his Kingdom, invisibly.

Nebuchadnezzar's madness is seen as a sort of punishment for taking the Jews into captivity, and by extension becomes the calculator by which the date of the Saviour's reappearance is arrived at.

Nebuchadnezzar's madness gave Russell a key date

William Miller

The prophet William Miller

Surprisingly, the story of the Seventh-Day Adventists does not begin with the observance of Saturday as the Lord's Day, but with a precise prophecy of the Second Coming, heralding the end of the world.

According to early Seventh-Day Adventist William Miller, Christ would return some time between 21 March 1843 and 21 March 1844.

Born in Pittsfield, Massachusetts in 1782, the young Miller underwent conversion, and after several years of intensive Bible study came to the conclusion that "in about twenty-five years from that time [1818] all the affairs of our present state would be wound up". Miller had found some interesting references to numbers in the Book of Daniel 9:24–27:

"24 Seventy weeks are determined upon thy people and upon thy holy city . . . and to anoint the most Holy.

25 Know therefore . . . that from the going forth of the commandment to restore and build [again] Jerusalem unto the Messiah the Prince shall be seven weeks, and three score and two weeks . . .

26 And after three score and two weeks shall Messiah be cut off . . . "

Miller took the starting date of this prophecy to be 457 BC, the year of the decree of Artaxerxes which permitted Ezra to return to Jerusalem and recommence worship in the Temple.

He understood one day in prophetic language to mean one year. Thus the 70 weeks mentioned in the text became 490 years. Miller promptly added 490 to 457 BC and was delighted when he got AD 33, the date of Christ's crucifixion. Now, he felt, he was definitely on the right track.

Miller then read Daniel 8:14:

"And he said unto me, Unto two thousand and three hundred days [literally 'evening morning']; then shall the sanctuary be cleansed [justified]."

Using the same formula as before, Miller established that the time period referred to was 2300 years. He added this number to 457 BC and got AD 1843. Reading further on, Daniel asks God for the meaning of this, and the Archangel Gabriel explains that "at the time of the end shall be the vision". Miller assumed then that, as AD 1843 was to be the end of the present order, the phrase "the sanctuary be cleansed"

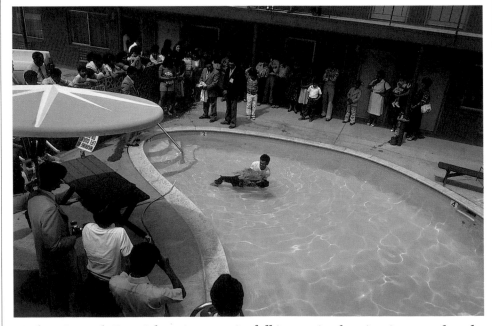

Modern Seventh-Day Adventists practise full immersion baptism in a motel pool

must indicate the return of Christ.

When the designated year arrived Christ did not return to reign on earth, and intense disappointment was felt among the Millerites, of whom there were by now many thousands. Miller himself was dumbfounded at the failure of his calculations. The year was moved forward to AD 1844 to take account of the BC/AD arithmetic anomaly (see panel). Again Christ failed to turn up. Then one of Miller's followers raised hopes again by suggesting that Christ's return would be not at the Equinox in 1844 but at the seventh month, specifically 22 October 1844, which corresponded to the Jewish Day of Atonement for that year. Miller accepted this new interpretation. Again they all waited, again in vain. The disappointment this time was overwhelming: 22 October is still referred to by Seventh-Day Adventists as "the Great Disappointment". Many people gave up the faith at this point, leaving only a small core of believers.

The movement was then rescued from oblivion by Hiram Edison. He claimed to have seen a vision which explained that the prophesied date was still valid, but that it represented the transference of the movement from one compartment of heaven to another! Joseph Bates, a retired sea captain, made a further contribution. In 1845 he became convinced that the seventh day of the week – when, according to Genesis, God rested – was Saturday. For centuries, he argued, Christians had been damning themselves by not observing the (correct) seventh day of rest. His reading of the Apocalypse of St John, chapter 7:4, was that only the 144,000 souls who correctly observed this Commandment would be saved at the end of the world.

But it is Ellen G. White (1827–1915) who can properly be credited with founding Seventh-Day Adventism as we recognize it today. She had roughly 200 visions, the contents of which were to do with both the Second Coming of Christ and the day-to-day theological problems of the new religion. White disseminated the ideas she received in these visions through the radio programme *The Voice of Prophecy*, the TV programme *Faith for Today* and a comprehensive list of publications.

Belief in the Second Coming of Christ is absolute among Adventists, although they no longer try to set a date for it. Some of their literature sets 1999 as the date for the end of the world, which will be brought about by the battle of Armageddon. All the wicked will perish in the battle, leaving the righteous, God's elect, to be transported to Heaven to rule with Christ for 1000 years, the new millennium.

At the end of this thousand years, Satan will be freed and the wicked dead allowed to rise from their graves and again overrun the earth. There will be yet another battle (not Armageddon) between Satan and his wicked hordes and Christ and his "camp of saints" in the newly descended New Jerusalem. Satan and his followers will eventually be annihilated.

WHAT MILLER'S CALCULATIONS RESTED UPON

Miller made several assumptions, all of them possibly flawed:

1 That a "day" in prophetic writings always equals a year, but 2300 days might literally mean 6.3 years rather than 2300 years.

2 That the 70 "weeks" and the 2300 "days" began at the same time. If, for example, the 2300 "days" ran from AD 33, then the date of Christ's Second Coming becomes AD 2333, not AD 1843.

3 That the correct baseline date was 457 BC. A case could be made for picking 445 or 444 BC instead, when permission was granted for the rebuilding of the walls of Jerusalem. Artaxerxes simply allowed Nehemiah and Ezra to return to Jerusalem in 457 BC.

4 That the "cleansing of the sanctuary" actually refers to Christ's coming, rather than some other pre-apocalyptic event.

5 Lastly, there is a small matter of arithmetic which has proved a stumbling block for many date calculations that cross from BC to AD. Because there were two "year ones" (AD 1 and BC 1), you must always remember to subtract one year from the first total arrived at. For example, the timespan between the beginning of January 2 BC and January AD 3 is not five years but four years.

This last error will be found in a number of other predictions discussed in this book, such as Gerald Massey's calculations.

The Burning Staircase

At noon on 19 April 1993, in Waco, Texas, David Koresh held fast with oratory 85 of his followers before luring them to a fiery grave with the promise of immortality.

Fire-obsessed "messiah" David Koresh

The Mount Carmel ranch at Waco

The men, women and children who perished with their mad "messiah" on this day were victims of a system of beliefs devised 150 years ago by William Miller.

Following the chronology of Archbishop Ussher, and interpreting the 2300 days of Daniel as 2300 years, Miller predicted that the end of the world would arrive in AD 1843. After one failed prophecy, Miller chose the "Seventh month" for the Advent of Christ, and on 22 October 1844 solemnly led his disciples up into the hills to meet their maker. As we know,

Christ did not arrive and his flock had to trudge back down again.

Some 90 years later, in 1931, a breakaway group from the mainstream of Seventh-Day Adventism, the self-styled Branch Davidian, established a centre at Waco. Since this time the sect has mainly recruited its members from the rank and file of Seventh-Day Adventists. The widow of the founder kept up his work until she died at the age of 85. In a frenzy of belief worthy of an Old Testament prophet the son dug up her body and declared that her successor was whoever could resurrect

the body. David Koresh, a member of the cult, pragmatically reported the son to the authorities. His subsequent arrest for unlawful exhumation resulted in a long stay in an institution.

The way was then clear for Koresh to take over leadership of the cult. He introduced a number of doctrines with strong sexual overtones. For him the anointing oil of the Psalms was symbolic of the sexual secretions of his female followers upon the head of his erect penis. He practised what he preached and insisted that chosen wives from among his followers should have sex with him and not their husbands. He also "marked" children of his followers as future wives; one such was Rachel Sylvia, who was 13 at the time she died in the inferno.

He wanted his followers to be one big happy family: he had two children with disciple Nicole Gent, three with Michelle Jones, one with Lorraine Sylvia and a further two with his wife Rachel – not to mention the numerous affairs he had with other followers. Theological threats of damnation were reinforced by physical punishment and subtle peer pressure.

Koresh believed that 1993 would herald the second coming of Christ, exactly some 150 years after Miller's original date. He prepared to separate his followers from the outside world. The ranch was fortified, secret tunnels were built and large amounts of semi-automatic weapons were bought by mail order. It was precisely these extensive postal purchases which first drew the attention of the gun law enforcement agency (ATF) to the sect. A request to search the premises was met with a hail of bullets which killed several agents. This rash act brought the weight of the law against the community. On 28 February 1993 a siege began, with Koresh refusing to allow either the law enforcement agencies to enter or his followers to leave the stronghold. Koresh often spoke of glorifying the Lord by dying in the fire. The FBI bombarded the compound with loud music, lit it with searchlights, and towed away Koresh's favourite car, a black Chevrolet.

Children who had been allowed to leave Mount Carmel, as the stronghold was called, told harrowing tales of physical and sexual abuse. Girls, some as young as 11, were given a symbolic star of David which signified that they had been selected to have sex with Koresh and must not be deflowered by any other member of the cult. These children were then taught to refer to Koresh as "father", and their natural parents as "dogs".

On the final day, 51 days after the siege first began, the FBI employed a tank as a battering ram to punch holes in the outer walls of the ranch. Inside Koresh calmed his followers, who put on gas masks and read from the Bible while CS gas rained on the compound. Those who attempted to leave were shot. Five hours later the 24 children, many of them his own, were separated from their parents and systematically drugged. Koresh sat in a reclining chair and read the Bible to the adults. The Apocalypse was now, he said, and they would pass to heaven with him through the purifying fire.

Finally, at 12.06 pm, Koresh gave the order to torch the kerosene that had been poured around the buildings and the ranch was engulfed by flames.

Ready for anything, except suicide: an "agent of Babylon" from the ATF squad

THE SECOND COMING OF CYRUS

The name "Koresh" means "sun" and is the Hebrew spelling of Cyrus, conqueror of Babylon, king and founder of Persia who lived in the 6th century BC. Koresh even called his son Cyrus, in honour of this king.

The original Cyrus was a polytheist, and perhaps a Zoroastrian or fire worshipper. His favourite form of punishment was burning his prisoners alive. King Cyrus allowed the Jews to leave Babylon and return to Palestine to rebuild the Temple of Jerusalem. The very favourable reference made to him in the Old Testament was to capture David Koresh's imagination.

If the FBI had been a bit more aware of Biblical history, they might have been able to foresee the fiery inferno which this latter day Cyrus had in store for his devoted followers.

Pregnant with the Messiah

Joanna Southcott, mother of Christ?

The prophet Joanna Southcott (1750–1814) experienced the Second Coming of Christ in a unique way, claiming that she was pregnant with the Messiah.

Born in Gittisham, Devon, into a tenant farming family, Joanna Southcott worked as a milkmaid and shopgirl before finding her real vocation as a prophet. An intensifying taste for religion and church-going made her reject carnal love and turn down suitors.

In 1792 she made her first prophecy, announcing during a Bible class that she was to be "the Lamb's wife". Then she had a fit and had to be carried out of the class. One day Joanna found a small seal with the initials "IC" and two stars on it. She adopted it as her own, interpreting the initials as those of Jesus Christ.

Joanna's big break came in January 1802 when she made the acquaintance of William Sharp, a wealthy engraver from Chiswick, west London, who became one of her disciples. Joanna moved to London, where she soon began to attract interest. The first Southcottian Chapel was opened in Duke Street, Southwark, by a dissenting West Country minister called William Tozer. Many in her growing audience "came to mock but remained to pray", according to one observer.

Eternal salvation would be granted to only 144,000 of her followers, Joanna declared. Furthermore, it was conditional upon them receiving the mark of the "IC" seal. A salvation document bearing the seal was accordingly offered to the faithful. This document stated that the recipient was "the sealed of the Lord . . . [and was] to inherit the tree of life – to be made heirs of God and joint-heirs with Jesus Christ"; in short, he or she owned a share in

paradise. Joanna issued at least 10,000 of these certificates, one of which was found in the possession of a murderess named Mary Bateman.

In late summer 1813, after a successful trip to northern England setting up new chapels, Joanna wrote letters to every bishop, peer, and Member of Parliament, as well as open letters to the London *Times* and other newspapers, announcing that she was soon to become the "mother of Shiloh". A

A cartoon of 1814, showing Joanna Southcott excommunicating the bishops

short while later she withdrew from public life, presumably to get on with her messianic pregnancy.

In March 1814 her disciples called in nine eminent doctors to examine the 64-year-old prophet. They all agreed that she showed unmistakeable signs of pregnancy and they estimated that the child would be born on Christmas Day. The news caused a great stir, and gifts of money, jewellery and clothing poured in from donors eager to cultivate the goodwill of the incipient second Jesus Christ.

However, on Christmas Day, growing weaker and beginning to feel that rather than giving birth to Christ she was in fact dying, Joanna gave her last instructions. Her body was to be kept warm, and then opened up four days after her death. The presents for the new Messiah were to be returned. Two days later she was dead. The autopsy showed no organic disease or foetus.

Surprisingly few of her followers seemed in the least disconcerted by the non-arrival of the Messiah and 50 years after her death, donations received

from her followers in just one city – Melbourne, Australia – enabled one of her disciples to build a mansion, Melbourne House, in Yorkshire.

This disciple was the bearded hunchback John Wroe. In 1823 he made two highly publicized attempts to walk on water, with predictable results. In the same year he had himself publicly circumcised. In the 1840s, after careful calculation, Wroe declared that the millennium would begin in 1863. His prophecy came true for him at least, as in that year he died.

THE MILLENNIAL PANDORA'S BOX

The secret box of the Panacea Society being X-rayed in 1927

One of Joanna Southcott's legacies to the world is a locked and sealed box tied with cords and still kept with great reverence in southern England. In it, or so her followers believe, is the secret of world peace, happiness and the millennium foretold in the Apocalypse of St John.

This box first came to light after the death of the Southcottians' then leader Helen Exeter, who had formed the Panacea Society to promote Joanna's writings. Like Wroe, she died in her predicted millennium year; she met her death in 1914, on a torpedoed ship in the English Channel. The box may only

be opened in the presence of the full complement of bishops of the Church of England, 24 of them in all, a stipulation that seems certain to keep it closed forever.

One man said to have opened the box was the famous psychical researcher Harry Price, in 1927. Among the strange assortment of items he discovered were an old nightcap, a flintlock pistol, some papers and a few odds and ends. The Panacea Society maintain that he cannot have opened Joanna's box.

In this last decade of the 20th century there are still groups of Southcottian believers dotted round the world who are awaiting the arrival of the millennium. This, they believe, will coincide with the opening of the mysterious box. Invoking Joanna's formula of "the fourth year after the first decade of the century", their estimated date of His arrival, and the millennium's, is 2014.

The Shining Virgin of Fatima

If you want to know what is going to happen at the end of the millennium from an impeccable source, then look no further than the prophecies of the Virgin Mary.

The light of the Virgin fell on the tree

On Sunday 13 May 1917, the Feast of the Ascension, Lucia, Francisco and Jacinta, children ranging in age from seven to ten, were tending sheep in a natural depression called Cova da Iria near the village of Fatima, about 80 miles (129 kilometres) north of Lisbon. Suddenly there was a startling flash of light in the clear sky. A second flash drew their eyes to a tree, in front of which stood a beautiful lady wearing a luminous white mantle and holding a coruscating rosary. She told the children not to be afraid and that she had come from Heaven. After asking them to return to the same spot at the same time on the thirteenth day of each of the next six months, the Lady rose into the sky and disappeared.

One month later the children went back to the same spot, this time accompanied by several incredulous villagers. At noon a small white cloud of light floated down from the sky and hovered above the same tree. Only the children saw the Lady, who prophesied that the eldest, Lucia Do Santos, would live to a ripe old age, whereas the other two would die soon, a prophecy which

came true. The Lady departed, and the villagers present claimed to have heard a sound like a rocket as the small cloud vanished into the sky.

The news spread rapidly, and for the Lady's third appearance, on 13 July, there were some 5000 people present. This time Lucia asked the Lady who she was. The Lady did not answer directly, but promised that World War I would end soon (it did the following year) and that "another, more terrible one will break out" during the reign of

Pope Pius XI, and would be heralded by an unknown light in the night sky.

This weird illumination of the sky occurred on 25 January 1938, when the skies of the northern hemisphere were filled with a crimson light, like "a reflection of the fires of hell". The *New York Times* devoted nearly a whole

The miraculous visitation of 13 October 1917 was observed by 70,000 people

page to this strange occurrence. Pope Pius XI was put under tremendous pressure by the dictators of Italy and Germany and died just before the out-break of World War II in 1939. The Lady said that the only way to prevent this second world war was for Russia to revert to Christianity, which as we know is just beginning to happen. After the reconversion and consecra-tion of Russia, she went on, "the world will be granted a period of peace".

The next promised appearance of the Lady, on 13 August 1917, was spoilt by the authorities, who arrested the three children. Some 15,000 people gathered at the spot and saw the white cloud of light appear from the east, hover for a time over the tree and then leave.

The appearance of 13 October drew a huge crowd of 70,000 people, roughly 17 per cent of the then popu-lation of the whole country. The day was overcast and at 10am it started to pour with rain. At half past one a pillar of smoke rose above the heads of the three children and evaporated; this happened three times. The clouds then parted to reveal a disk (some said this was the sun) which shone like dull silver. This disk could be stared at without pain to the eyes or blinding. It began to whirl around and as it did so a succession of glowing colours passed over its surface. The atmosphere changed to a purple colour and then to "the colour of old yellow damask".

So what was this event – a miracle or a figment of the imagination? From the subsequent testimony of thousands, it is certain that something incredible did happen and that it cannot be explained as a "trick of the light", a hoax, or indeed a climatic aberration.

Pilgrims came to Fatima in their thousands

THE VIRGIN SPEAKS OUT

Great controversy surrounds the third of the prophecies of the Virgin. Lucia, it is said, turned white on hearing it and cried out in fear. She refused to disclose the contents of the prophecy, but eventually wrote it down and sent it to the Pope via the Bishop of Leiria.

Although part of the prophecy was released to the world in 1942 by Pope Pius XII, mainly that concern-ing the war, the rest of it has not been disclosed. There are fairly com-pelling reasons for believing that the rest of the prophecy predicts the per-secution of the Pope and ultimate destruction of the Roman Catholic Church in about the year 2000. No wonder it is still suppressed by the Vatican, despite the Lady's instruc-tion that it could, and should, be fully revealed to the public in 1960.

A Stuttgart newspaper, the *Neues Europa*, had no doubt that this was indeed the content of the third prophecy. On 15 October 1963, the newspaper printed what they claimed to be the text of the prophecy:

"For the Church too, the time of its greatest trial will come. Cardinals will oppose cardinals and bishops against bishops. Satan will march in their midst and there will be great changes at Rome. What is rotten will fall, never to rise again. The church will be darkened and the world will shake with terror. The time will come when no king, emperor, cardinal or bishop will await Him who will, however, come, but in order to punish according to the designs of my Father."

Mr Donnelly's Truths Held Dear

American Congressman Ignatius Donnelly did not succeed in convincing many people with his strange, heretical theories of lost worlds, but he certainly knew how to attract attention to them.

Born on 3 November 1831 to a middle-class migrant Irish family settled in Philadelphia, Donnelly trained as a lawyer before going into politics at the age of 24. By 1859 he was Lieutenant-Governor of Minnesota, despite an attempt to found a model city which had ended in bankruptcy. In public life he was a great orator and rabble-rouser, quick to denounce scandals, rackets and conspiracies.

Apart from his politicking, Donnelly is remembered for coming up with three improbable theories. The first concerns the destruction of the lost city of Atlantis, which is said by some to have sunk beneath the waves of the Atlantic. Not since the time of Plato had this myth held much interest for the rest of the world. After Donnelly's re-heating, it is doubtful if Plato would have recognized it. In his book *Atlantis: the Antediluvian World*, Donnelly tried to put right what he saw as the total corruption of history. The end-product was a model of how to make very flimsy evidence seem very substantial, and almost believable.

Donnelly identified Atlantis as the origin of such locations as the Garden of Eden, Garden of the Hesperides, Elysian Fields, Mount Olympus, Asgard, and virtually every other paradise dreamt about by man. After the deluge (which became the prototype of flood myths in many cultures) and destruction of this earthly paradise, Atlantean colonists were supposed to have initiated cultures in Egypt, America, and that of the Aryan and

The supposed location of Atlantis

Semitic cultures. How else, Donnelly argued, can we explain the religious use of pyramids in both Central America, in the Inca culture, and in ancient Egyptian culture? These cultures must have sprung from the same, shared mid-Atlantic origin. In a word, Atlantis.

Donnelly's work was not simply disregarded as the ravings of a madman. No less a person than the British prime minister Gladstone tabled a motion in the House of Commons proposing that a Royal Navy task force be sent to the Atlantic to search for remnants of Atlantis. Harder heads in the Treasury vetoed this idea on the grounds of cost.

Not content to rest on these laurels, Donnelly then busied himself with theories concerning the destruction of the world, published in his book *Ragnarok*. The *London Daily News* referred to its author as "a stupendous speculator in cosmogony". Donnelly's visionary tone soon won many admirers for his grandiose notions. He theorized that a giant comet had almost, and indeed still could, bring death and destruction to Earth. Later, Immanuel Velikovsky was to expand these theories, giving them a scientific basis, and, amazingly, make scientific predictions from them which would later be proved correct.

Tiring perhaps of writing about the past, Donnelly made an attempt at predicting the events of the 1990s in a book he called *Caesar's Column*, published in 1890. He accurately predicted the supremacy of big business over morality and politics, but the notion that large cities would be powered by the earth's magnetic currents seems a long way from being realized.

Donnelly envisaged modern cities at the end of the 20th century relying heavily on slave labour. In Donnelly's book this under-class eventually revolts, destroying the state armies by aerial bombardment and massacring the ruling classes. The victims of the revolt are cemented into a huge pillar of concrete to commemorate the revolution, then the mob turns on its leaders and lynches them as well. The hero of the book escapes from New York in an airship and flies to Europe. From Europe he flees south, taking with him the people who will found a new civilization in, of all places, Uganda.

After being elected Vice-President of the People's Party in the United States, Donnelly took a second wife, who was 46 years younger than himself. He died peacefully in 1901.

Were Mexican pyramids a remnant from the once glorious civilization of Atlantis?

Restaurants would serve every imaginable dish from all over the world, cooked at the press of a button, which is a good guess at the technology of the microwave. News from any part of the globe would also be available at the press of a button and would be shown on individual screens, an amazingly accurate prophecy of current computer-based news technology.

SHAKESPEARE'S SECRETS

The crowning achievement of Donnelly's life, or so he felt, was his "deciphering" of Shakespeare. In this he followed an earlier American, Delia Bacon, who hoped to restore credit for William Shakespeare's plays to her namesake, Francis Bacon. This research involved incredibly tortuous manipulations of the text and its corresponding numerical values, which were designed to yield hidden messages from Bacon, the supposed secret author of Shakespeare's works.

Bacon's well-known penchant for ciphers made him a natural choice for the author of an immensely complex body of plays from which all kinds of messages could be extracted with the exercise of a little imagination. Donnelly, however, was not interested in applying a little imagination, and in the course of these intricate researches he claimed to have used up two tons of paper. His monumental work, *The Great Cryptogram*, runs to almost 1000 pages. Unfortunately, it amply demonstrates to what level a once great intellect can fall.

The second volume reduced Donnelly to a laughing stock in intellectual circles, from which a lesser man would never have recovered. Perhaps, though, he had the last laugh: the book sold out, was reprinted, and was soon followed by a sequel on the same subject.

Francis Bacon, the great bard?

The Christian Israelites

Once it was thought that the most expedient way to bring forward the date of the millennium was to cause the appearance of the predicted signs of the Apocalyse.

One of the most important signs of the coming Apocalypse was the return of the dispersed Jews to Israel, and, according to some interpreters, their conversion to Christianity.

As early as the 4th century AD the Tibertine Oracle, the first of the forged medieval Sibylline Oracles, prophesied the Jews' eventual acceptance of Christ. In medieval Europe the persecution of Jews who refused conversion often went hand-in-hand with the Crusades for the recovery of the Holy

Richard Brothers

Land. Pope Paul IV established Rome's Jewish ghetto in 1555 to facilitate originally well-intentioned conversion efforts.

The cult of Anglo-Israelitism emerged in England with Puritanism, which took literally the Bible's prophecies of the restoration of Israel, and now flourishes predominantly in the USA. Under the Puritan government of Oliver Cromwell in the 1650s the laws against Jewish immigration were relaxed, although not completely lifted. So curious were Cromwell's views of the Jewish people that the Jewish community in the Netherlands went so far as to send an investigator to check if Cromwell's roots were actually Jewish.

In recognition of their religious roots, one particularly fanatical Puritan, Praisegod Barebone, was in the forefront of moves by the Little Parliament (1653) to abolish the English constitution and replace it with the Jewish laws of Moses.

This was taken to a crazy extreme in the late 18th century by Richard Brothers (1757–1824), a retired naval

Oliver Cromwell

officer who proclaimed himself the King of the Jews. He believed that he and his followers had been divinely chosen to lead the Jews back to the Holy Land and lodge them in a splendid New Jerusalem before converting them to Christianity in preparation for the second coming of the Messiah.

Brothers told of visionary, and highly improbable, experiences, such as seeing the Devil walking down a London street and receiving two angels at his lodging house. Eventually the authorities tired of his rantings and had him committed to a lunatic asylum.

Before the Jews could be returned to Israel, there was the small problem of locating the ten so-called lost tribes of Israel. These tribes were captured by the Assyrians and dispersed from Palestine in the 8th century BC, leaving just the two tribes of the kingdom of Judaea. Several scholars, including Edward Hine (1801–85), "discovered" that, after long wanderings, these ten tribes had ended their journey in England.

Isaiah himself lent some credence to this idea when he said that "the Lord shall . . . recover the remnant of his people, which shall be left, from Assyria, and from Egypt . . . and from the islands of the sea" (11:11). Hine concluded that these islands were certainly the British Isles. Hine's idea drew support from Professor Piazzi Smyth, Astronomer Royal for Scotland, who had a few odd theories of his own regarding the Great Pyramid.

Anthony Cooper, the seventh Earl of Shaftesbury (1801–85), President of the Society for Promoting Christianity among the Jews, strove to bring about the Second Coming by converting the Jews. Described as the "prince of do-gooders", Cooper was famous for his reformation of the working conditions of Victorian chimneysweeps. He even arranged an emigration service for London's leading thieves. Cooper had less success with his conversion plan: his best year saw only three conversions. Strangely, most of his converts were rabbis!

Successive British governments were committed to the principle of a new Jewish homeland by the Balfour Declaration of 1917. Finally, in May 1948, this intention was translated into the establishment of the state of Israel. Interestingly, the sum total of the numbers in this date (1+9+4+8) comes to 22, the number of letters in the Hebrew alphabet and a mystical number in the Jewish qabalah.

BRITISH ISRAELITES IN AMERICA

The Puritan settlers took their identification with the Jews to America with them. In the 19th century Edward Hine was among those who tried to keep the message alive there, in 1884 undertaking an extended speaking tour of the States. After several years of itinerant prophesying he fell on hard times and had to be repatriated to his homeland by his British followers.

The promised restoration of the Jews to Palestine loomed large in US prophecy conferences held between 1878 and 1918. When the state of Israel was founded a teacher at the Bible Institute of Los Angeles announced on radio that this was "the greatest piece of prophetic news that we have had in the 20th century". Jesus was expected to come at any moment.

A similar reaction greeted Israel's capture of the Old City of Jerusalem during the Six Day War in 1967, which seemed to confirm centuries of prophetic speculation. Hal Lindsey's *Late Great Planet Earth*, which came out three years later, sold in vast numbers on the back of a fresh resurgence of interest in millennial prophecies.

Of the post-War American proponents of Anglo-Israelism, James Lovell (of Kingdon Digest), Howard Rand (of Destiny Publishers) and Herbert W. Armstrong are perhaps the best known. Armstrong, founder of the Radio Church of God, editor of *The Plain Truth* magazine and veteran of religious programmes on television, concerned himself particularly with Anglo-Israelism and millennial prophecy.

The departure of Puritans from Delft to join the Mayflower *voyage*

Sister Marie Gabriel's Warning

On Monday 19 July 1993, Sister Marie Gabriel Paprocski, a "secular plain clothes religious Sister" with an interest in astronomy, let it be known that a gigantic comet was on a collision course with Jupiter.

According to this Polish nun's calculations, a comet would collide with Jupiter before 25 July 1994. Her prediction contradicted Velikovsky's notion of a massive body having been torn out of Jupiter 3500 years ago.

Sister Marie Gabriel's warning came in a letter addressed to all world leaders, including Pope John Paul II, President Bill Clinton and President Yeltsin of the CIS. Press releases were sent to the major television companies and full-page adverts were taken in the major international newspapers. The good Sister certainly went to some trouble to promote her prophecy.

Sister Marie Gabriel, who claims to be the "astronomer Sophia", first made known her prediction in July 1986. The collision between Jupiter and the comet would, she said, produce the "biggest cosmic explosion in the history of mankind". Although at the time her description of the comet as "a fireball asteroid" persuaded many astronomers to dismiss her pronouncement as the ravings of a publicity seeking crackpot, subsequently scientists themselves predicted that a collision between Jupiter and a comet was indeed on the cards, albeit with no catastrophic fallout for mankind.

Sister Marie Gabriel's Biblical precedent for her prophecy is Isaiah 24:1, where the prophet says "behold, the Lord maketh the earth empty, and maketh it waste, and turneth it upside down, and scattereth abroad the inhabitants thereof". Again, in Isaiah 24:18 there is a strange passage predicting natural upheavals of an unpleasant sort: "the windows from on high are open, and the foundations of the earth do shake", which sounds very much as if something loosed from the heavens has shaken the earth from its orbit, or at the very least caused earthquakes.

Finally, Isaiah 24:19–20 depicts the scene after the catastrophe, when "the earth is utterly broken down, the earth is clean dissolved, the earth is moved exceedingly. The earth shall reel to and fro like a drunkard". Presented here is a clear picture of the Earth being thrown off its normal path by the impact of the comet hitting Jupiter.

In the time-honoured fashion of prophets, Sister Marie Gabriel explained this cosmic event as a warning from God to all governments,

Halley's Comet, benign compared to the comet due to collide with Jupiter in 1994

A solar eclipse could reveal a comet

to do His bidding swiftly and adopt the following eight measures:

1 Drastically reduce crime rates by copying Saudi Arabia's system of law and order.

2 Destroy all pornographic material.

3 Ban crime and indecency from TV.

4 The UK government was specifically enjoined to prevent the National Health Service killing off older patients in order to make room for more patients in its hospitals.

5 Ban all alcohol.

6 Compel women to observe an almost Muslim dress code.

7 Ban all animal cruelty, specifically the shooting of birds in Italy and Spain, trapping, bullfighting, etc.

8 End all wars.

However, Sister Marie Gabriel did not make clear the connection between changes in human morals and astronomical movements.

Asteroids as well as comets do pose a threat to our planet if they are large enough to survive the plunge through the Earth's atmosphere and reach the surface. Sister Marie might have been thinking of one such recent visitor to the Earth's atmosphere which changed its mind and left again just two months before she publicized her prediction.

This asteroid, estimated as measuring about 30 feet (9.2 metres) in diameter and weighing the equivalent of a navy destroyer, passed within 90,000 miles (140,000 kilometres) of Earth on 20 May 1993. The asteroid was reckoned to be travelling at about 48,000 mph (77,000 km/hr) so this distance, which represents less than half the distance between the Earth and the Moon, would soon have been gobbled up if it had survived the fiery plunge through the atmosphere. This near-miss went unnoticed until the asteroid was detected as it whizzed away from the Earth's atmosphere. It would have made a very large crater indeed if it had reached our planet.

1066 AND ALL THAT

The appearance of a comet was long believed to indicate the arrival of some cataclysmic event. Of all the heavenly phenomena, comets were perhaps the easiest to observe after eclipses, which were also meant to have significance for mankind. A comet was seen before William the Conqueror's invasion of England in 1066, a fact commemorated in the Bayeux Tapestry, where it is depicted as a star on a stick connected to what appear to be flames.

It is no wonder that the writer Erich von Daniken used this type of image to boost his flying saucer theory, as the depiction in the Tapestry gives a clearer idea of a comet than is afforded by looking through a telescope. The comet seen in 1066 could be said to have heralded the birth of England as a nation. Sister Marie Gabriel's comet seemed to signal the nation's demise.

Before the 18th century and the age of reason, events like the eclipse of the Sun or Moon were widely thought to presage important events in life. The precise nature of these events was open to interpretation. Not surprisingly, the paranoid drew little comfort from them. Pope Urban VIII, for example, was on tenterhooks from about the time of the eclipse of the Moon in January 1628 through the eclipse of the Sun in December 1628 and June 1630, such was his conviction that any of these events might be forewarnings of his death. He even engaged the services of a heretic and sorcerer, Tommasso Campanella, to help him avert the perceived danger.

Campanella had been condemned to life imprisonment after attempting to establish a Utopia and "provoke" the millennium. To secure the safety of his prestigious client, Campanella performed elaborate black arts rituals during the periods of eclipse. It is quite amusing to think of a Pope so desperate to cling to the mortal coil that he would employ for his own ends the same ungodly practices that he was trying to stamp out in the general populace.

Self-made Messiahs

Some relatively modern-day prophets of the Apocalypse have crossed the thin line dividing prophecy from theophany, and have claimed to actually be the Messiah.

Haile Selassie, Lion of Judah

Prophets declaring themselves to be the Messiah is not an unusual phenomenon, and in the Middle Ages there was no shortage of Christian, Jewish and even Muslim claims to the title.

Two extraordinary messiahs of the 19th century were Henry James Prince (1811–99) and John Hugh Smyth-Pigott (d. 1927). Prince was an Anglican priest with a gift for great oratory and for attracting women. He became convinced that his sermons owed their force to the Holy Spirit. Prince took to preaching in the open, and soon announced that he was, in fact, the prophet Elijah reincarnated. He established his own chapel in the English south-coast resort of Brighton.

Enough people of means believed in Prince to buy him a large house with some 200 acres (81 hectares) of land at Spraxton in Somerset. There, in 1846, he established the "Abode of Love", or Agapemone. The group soon became known as the Agapemonites (from the Greek word for love). Prince took the title of "the Beloved One" and, eventually, "the Messiah".

As he was the will of God on earth, Prince suffered no questions from his disciples about the luxurious lifestyle he enjoyed at their expense. On at least one occasion he drove in his carriage through the Somerset town of Bridgewater with his footman sounding a trumpet and proclaiming him as the Messiah. Soon he began taking successive disciples as his "bride of the Lamb", a feature of his "church" which other cult leaders, like David Koresh of Waco for example, would later emulate.

Prince was "above sin" and so free to live as he pleased. Not so his followers, who were expected to lead chaste lives. This double standard did not deter believers and even when funds ran low the needs of the Messiah were

The Taiping rebellion, a plot to establish China as the Promised Land

met. One wealthy merchant contributed all his worldly goods, amounting to £10,000 ($15,000), a large sum in those days, and came to work in the Abode of Love as a butler.

The facts of the ex-Anglican priest's defrocking and several lawsuits – brought by families keen to prevent relatives handing over money and possessions – did not harm his cause, and the Abode of Love flourished. It even raised the funds to build a Church of the Ark of the Covenant in Clapton, London. Believing the end of the world to be nigh, Prince granted his followers immortality. Those who died had "lapsed into sin", and were buried standing up under the lawn, a fate which awaited Prince himself in 1899.

Three years later the spiritual vacuum left by Prince's death was filled by John Smyth-Pigott, who

Smyth-Pigott, Abode of Love Messiah

THE LION OF JUDAH IN AFRICA

One of the most extraordinary messianic movements of the present day is Rastafarianism, which has spread from Jamaica to the US and UK. The involuntary candidate for the messiahship was the Emperor of Ethiopia, Haile Selassie (1891–1975).

Rastafarianism took its cue from the rhetoric of the militant pro-Negro Marcus Garvey during World War I. Garvey, a Jamaican emigrant to the USA, wanted to be the political saviour of all black people, and was strongly anti-white. He maintained that Negroes should look to Africa "when a black king shall be crowned, for deliverance is near". Soon afterwards, in 1930, Ras Tafari became the Emperor of Ethiopia, Haile Selassie, the fulfilment of Garvey's prophecy. Haile Selassie, who assumed the title "Lion of Judah", became the last in what he claimed to be the longest unbroken monarchy in the world.

Some of the more extreme Rastafarians, such as the Niyamen, advocated the use of marijuana (ganja), grew 'dreadlocks', and promoted a militantly anti-white stance. A sort of cargo cult grew up around their expectation of a wholesale migration to a new kingdom in Africa, and fortunes were made on the sale of worthless tickets and passports.

The Rastafarians have survived this disappointment and the death of Haile Selassie in 1975. Like the Jews of past generations, they have a homeland which is not recognized as theirs. Visions of the return of either Haile Selassie or another black Messiah coupled with the possibility of an Armageddon which might also entail a race war continues to feed Rastafarian expectations. This vision of a racial Armageddon was later to fuel Charles Manson's murderous campaign in California.

declared himself "the Son of Man", the new Messiah, at the Clapton church. He continued Prince's practice of selecting "soul brides", who also bore his children. This eventually led to his defrocking as an Anglican clergyman. At any one time, there were as many as 100 women at the Abode of Love.

Prince and Smyth-Pigott had comfortable lives in comparison with some other "Messiahs", perhaps because comparatively few people took them seriously. The Chinese prophet and military leader Hung Hsui-chaun, on the other hand, stirred up a hornet's nest when he claimed to be the younger brother of Christ. His declaration inspired the Taiping rebellion, which began in southern China in 1851 and lasted until 1864. His followers thought they were the children of Israel and sought to overthrow the Manchu dynasty in order to establish China as the promised land. The British General Gordon suppressed the revolution; in Sudan in the 1880s he would also oppose the Mahdi, a Muslim claimant to the title of Messiah.

The
AQUARIAN
AGE

*Has the dawning of this Age sounded the
death knell for Christianity, and are we
going forward into a strange New Age
based on peace, love and the exploration
of the drug-accessed depths of our inner
space? Embracing the philosophy of the
New Age may be our only defence against
the horrors of the Apocalypse.*

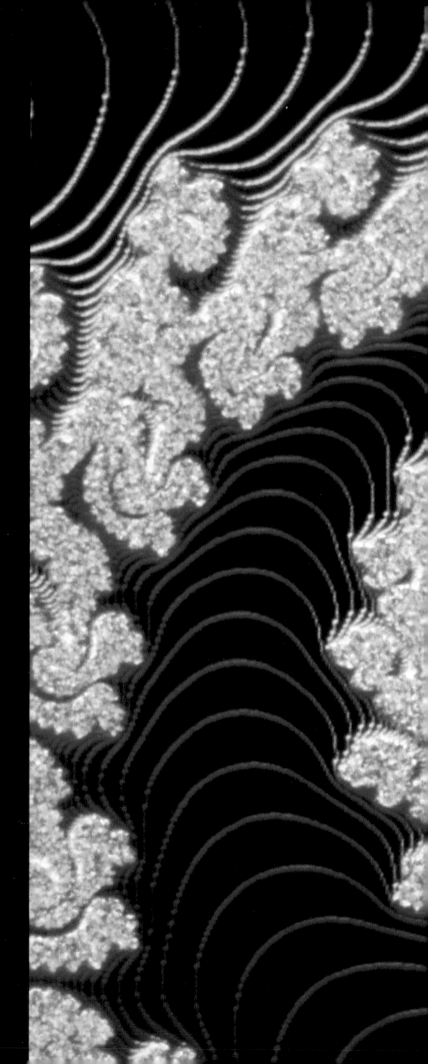

Madame Blavatsky

In 1888, Helena Petrovna Blavatsky (1831–91), the founder of theosophy, claimed that Lemuria was the home of the "third root race".

HPB, the Russian Sphinx

HPB, as she was known by her disciples, was born in the Ukraine as Helena Petrovna von Hahn, the daughter of a Russian army officer of German extraction. In 1849 she married General Blavatsky, the vice-governor of Erivan, but soon afterwards took to wandering the world.

Lemuria was a lost continent believed by some to have existed in the Indian or Pacific Oceans until it was destroyed by a volcanic eruption. According to Theosophists, the human species evolved through a number of root races. Among these were the Lemurians, who came before the Atlanteans and the current human species (the "fifth root race").

The name Lemuria was originally taken from the monkey-like lemur, which is found in Africa, south India and Malaysia. The wide distribution of these habitats caused scientists as distinguished as Thomas Huxley and Ernst Haeckel to believe that a continent must have once linked them. This conjecture by 19th-century naturalists looking for an Asian-African land bridge was soon hijacked by a group of

people intent on finding a likely location for a rather less plausible theory.

Their Lemuria was the cradle of human civilization – the Garden of Eden, no less. The original inhabitants of Lemuria were, according to Madame Blavatsky, hermaphroditic, egg-laying, four-armed and three-eyed (like some Hindu gods) ape-like giants. Fortunately for us, beings from Venus offered to replace them and interbred with the local apes, a Darwinian touch. The irony is that scientists no longer believe that there was a bridging continent called Lemuria.

Madame Blavatsky said that the third root race of Lemuria was swept away more than 40 million years ago, although their descendants survive as Australian Aborigines, Papuans and Hottentots – a theory that it would be hard to persuade a modern anthropologist to accept. Perhaps stories of the Lemurians' incredible height were borrowed from descriptions of the supposedly very tall Tasmanian Aborigines, who were safely extinct by the time Blavatsky was writing. This

height myth derived from the distances between step-cuts made by Tasmanian Aborigines when climbing trees.

After the death of Madame Blavatsky in 1891, the cause was taken up by her successor, Annie Besant, a tireless fighter for social justice. Together with W. Scott-Elliot, she elaborated on the history of Lemuria, and even provided detailed maps showing critical stages of the world's evolution. These bear more than a passing resemblance to the current maps of "Pangaea", a modern myth with which modern science attempts to document continental drift.

The fourth root race were supposed to live in Atlantis, where they developed a technology that was propelled by concentrated willpower. Finally

Atlantis was destroyed, according to Plato's commentary on this civilization, possibly by the eruption of the volcano Santorini.

The fifth root race, the Aryans, evolved from Atlantis and settled in Egypt, India, Persia and Europe. From there they spread, as history records, in the last four centuries to most corners of the earth.

The sixth root race are said to be just beginning to develop in California, following on from the arrival of the new World Teacher or Messiah (see panel). This race will develop steadily over many thousands of years and eventually displace the present race.

Life on earth will end with the seventh root race, at which point, according to Madame Blavatsky's Masters, it will begin again on the planet Mercury. This idea of life transferring to another planet was a theme also dear to the hearts of the Aetherians.

A contemporary view of M. Blavatsky

KRISHNAMURTI: MESSIAH OF A NEW AGE

Theosophists subscribed to the Hindu doctrine of avatars which held that God incarnated himself as a man when it was necessary to advance evolution. The Society felt the time was ripe for a new incarnation, and started actively looking for one. In 1908 members of the Theosophical Society noticed a local boy watching them swimming in the Adyar river. Two members, Ernest Wood and the Reverend C. W. Leadbeater, noticed that this 13-year-old was possessed of an exceptional aura. After looking into his past lives, as they put it, they suggested to the boy's father that the Theosophical Society should take charge of his education.

The boy's name was Jiddu Krishnamurti. After several legal tussles with Krishnamurti senior, who was an orthodox Hindu, the Theosophical Society started to promote Krishnamurti as a new World Teacher, almost a new Messiah.

In 1911 the Society proclaimed that Krishnamurti was the channel for the wisdom of the Lord Maitreya, or the fifth and last incarnation of the Buddha, and decided that 1911 signalled the initiation of the Age of Aquarius.

Krishnamurti was then taken on a world tour in order to meet the faithful. In Sydney, Australia, Theosophists even went to the trouble and expense of building a huge amphitheatre by the Harbour from which they could greet the new Messiah, or, as they preferred to call him, the World Teacher.

In 1927 Krishnamurti underwent a profound experience which changed his relationship with the Theosophical Society. He felt he had been admitted to the ranks of "the Beloved" and accepted his dharma as a teacher, and this awareness prompted him to break away from the Society. In 1929 Krishnamurti rejected his role as a Theosophical guru, renounced his title of Messiah and made a new base at Ojai in California. His lectures on philosophy and the spiritual life were instrumental in developing the consciousness which would lead to the new Age of Aquarius proclaimed by the hippies in the early 1960s. Maybe they are the progenitors of Madame Blavatsky's sixth root race.

Krishnamurti, the boy beside the river

The Prophet of the New Age

The reputation of the prophet Aleister Crowley was made by the publication of his seminal The Book of the Law, *the contents of which had been given to him by one of the old Egyptian daemons.*

Prophet as well as magician and poet?

The entity which called on Crowley and his wife Rose in their Cairo apartment in the spring of 1904 was named Aiwass. It foretold the end of Christianity and the birth of a new age, a transition that would be marked by violence, force, fire and destruction.

The Book of the Law, or "Liber Al vel Legis", appeared as a short prose

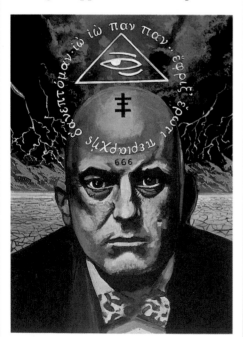

Aleister Crowley and all-seeing eye

poem in three chapters. On its publication Crowley was heralded as the prophet of a new age, "the Aeon of the Crowned and Conquering Child" of Horus, the Egyptian hawk-god of war.

The rule of this new Aeon was similar to that of Rabelais' dictum, "There is no law beyond do what thou wilt". This was not meant as a licence to behave as you pleased. (He was rediscovered 20 years later by the hippie movement who found in his philosophy many parallels with their own attitudes and beliefs.) Crowley meant that each individual should try to find purpose in his or her life: in short, to discover what was their True Will. They should then strive to do only this, and not be bound by the fetters of conventional morality, or go through the time-wasting motions of "acceptable" but false behaviour.

When Crowley died in 1947 he was mourned by only a small band of disciples. Twenty years later publishers were reprinting all his books and his image was used prominently on the cover of the Beatles' album *Sergeant Pepper's Lonely Hearts Club Band*.

But what of Crowley's prophecies? Crowley was later to claim that not only did *The Book of the Law* prophesy the coming of war and bloodshed, but that it actually precipitated it. With each authorized edition of the book, the transition to the new Aeon was brought one step closer.

In the 46th verse of the third chapter are the prophetic words "I am the warrior Lord of the Forties". Crowley recorded that he did not understand this phrase when he wrote it, but read in the light of knowledge of World War II it seems shockingly clear.

If this still strikes you as pure coincidence, then consider one of Crowley's experiments with ritual magic. In 1910, while staying at the home of his friend and pupil Commander Marston, a former officer in the Royal Navy, Crowley agreed to invoke Bartzabel, the spirit of Mars, the god of war.

Victor Neuberg acted as medium; this means that he allowed Bartzabel to speak through him to prophesy and answer questions. The invocation was duly performed, using a ritual written by Crowley, and Victor began to speak the words of the Spirit of Mars. Commander Marston asked Bartzabel about the possibilities of an outbreak of war in Europe.

The spirit replied that within five years [from 1910] there would be two conflicts; the storm centre of the first would be Turkey and the second would be the German Empire. The result of these wars would be the destruction of the Turkish and German empires. Both these prophecies were fulfilled to the letter by the Balkan War of 1912 and World War I.

Crowley's book points to war in Europe in the year 1997; several of its coded passages refer to the 93 years to be added to its date of origination, 1904, giving April 1997 as a commencement (or completion) date of war. This conflict will spread through Eastern Europe or the newly independent states of the former Soviet Union. For the end of this century we must "expect the direful judgements of Ra-Hoor-Khuit! This shall regenerate the world". Ra-Hoor-Khuit, another Egyptian god of war, will help in the changeover from one Aeon to another at the end of the century.

The Book of the Law then foretells: "Hrumachis shall arise and the double-wanded one assume my throne and place. Another prophet shall arise, and bring fresh fever from the skies . . . another sacrifice shall stain the tomb; another king shall reign". (Hrumachis is the Dawning Sun of the new Aeon. The "double-wanded one" is the Egyptian god from whom the Greeks derived Themis, goddess of justice.)

"Invoke me under my stars! Love is the law, love under wil ...take wine and strange drugs . . . & be drunk thereof! They shall not harm ye at all" – a passage summing up the psychedelic love-ins of the 1960s, which it would have been hard to imagine in 1904! Crowley's book is certainly a powerful piece of prophetic literature, filled with love, and hate.

THE SECRET KEY

Book 2:76 of *The Book of the Law* contains a series of apparently disconnected letters and numbers. Crowley explained the purpose of these: "This passage following appears to be a Qabalistic test . . . of any person who may claim to be the Magical Heir of The Beast". Crowley had adopted the title of "Beast 666" from his favourite Biblical book, the Apocalypse of St John.

So far, despite many attempts, nobody has publicly come up with really clear and convincing proof that they can untangle this "key", thereby proving themselves to be Crowley's spiritual successors. Charles Stansfield Jones claimed to have sorted it out, but Crowley later decided that his explanation had not got to the bottom of the puzzle. The puzzle is this:

4 6 3 8 A B K 2 4 a L G M O R 3 Y
X 24 89 R P S T O V A L

At first glance this is so much nonsense, but by the application of the word to letter equivalency of the Qabalah, it begins to make some sense. It is worth noting that the "G" above is not really a "G" but symbolizes something else. Maybe the prophet who succeeds in cracking this will also come up with some explanations for the rest of the prophecies in Crowley's strange book.

The Egyptian god of war Ra-Hoor-Khuit may have had a hand in two world wars.

The Sleeping Prophet

Edgar Cayce (1877–1945), the so-called "sleeping prophet", made a number of remarkably accurate predictions and an almost equal number of wildly inaccurate ones.

Edgar Cayce, healer and prophet

Cayce realized at an early age that he had psychic powers, but it was only later in life that he would specialize in the trance diagnosis for which he became famous. What sets Cayce apart from most prophets is that his readings were carefully transcribed and kept in an archive which still survives.

During consultation with his patients he would lie down on a couch, make himself comfortable, and then allow his inner light to connect him with his "channel" of communication. He would then "read" off the diagnosis and solution to the condition or problem. When he awoke he claimed to remember nothing of what had been spoken through him.

Although poorly educated in the traditional sense, in trance Cayce often diagnosed illnesses, described conditions accurately, and prescribed detailed treatments and medicines in terms which suggested formal training as a doctor. He was not always right, and handed back his fee to anyone who was not happy with his "readings".

Once Cayce prescribed a remedy prepared from the plant clary, but no one could trace it. Eventually the patient, James Andrews, discovered that a doctor in Paris had marketed such a remedy 60 years previously. Cynics could argue that Cayce had been reading old medical manuals, but for the following case.

On this occasion he recommended the use of a drug called "Codiron", giving the name and address of the manufacturing chemists who could supply it. When the patient telephoned the firm in Chicago he found that the formula for the medicine had only just been established and its actual name chosen barely an hour before his call! Cayce's "channel of communication" would later save the sight of his

Cayce predicted the 1991–2 eruptions of the active volcano Mount Etna

eight-year-old son, who had damaged his eyes while playing with matches. The specialist wanted to remove one eye. Cayce forbade the operation and sought his own counsel. Bandages steeped in tannic acid – the remedy given to Cayce during one of his trances – were placed on his son's eyes. In a fortnight the boy could see again.

In everyday life Cayce ran a photographer's shop in Virginia Beach, Virginia. As well as helping people with medical problems, Cayce was also able to use his psychic talents to give business advice. These forecasts were highly regarded by those who came to see him and profited from them. One man who sought his advice on 5 March 1929 was told not to invest in stocks and shares. Cayce gave similar advice on 6 April and described "a downward movement of long duration", just before the Wall Street crash of 1929.

Cayce predicted the end of Communism, and that Russia would be born again. He also saw a strong

The predicted earthquake in Turkey

religious movement coming out of Russia. A less plausible prediction was that China will become the new "cradle of Christianity".

In 1934 Cayce made a series of pronouncements about major geological and climatic changes (see below). An eruption of Mount Etna was predicted – it last erupted destructively in 1991, destroying the village of Fornazzo, and again the following year. He also predicted an eruption on Vesuvius (near Naples in Italy) or Mount Pelée in Martinique, the last mentioned triggering earthquake activity in southern California. In 1999 the shift in the earth's axis, which began in 1936 according to Cayce, will cause a number of catastrophes. The year 2000 is scheduled to arrive with a bang, with major earthquakes in Turkey and the Balkans, causing areas of the land to disappear under the sea. The only positive occurrence would seem to be a climatic change for the better in Scandinavia and Britain as a result of an alteration to the Gulf Stream!

Like many Christian prophets, Cayce maintained that "the day of reckoning" was at hand. He predicted the arrival of World War III in 1999, followed by the New Age and the Second Coming of Christ. Cayce saw himself reincarnating in Nebraska in AD 2100 – he may then be able to check on his various predictions.

MAJOR UPHEAVALS DUE AT THE END OF THE CENTURY

In 1934 Cayce gave a trance "reading" which described a number of quite unimaginable natural catastrophes that would occur at the end of the 20th century. These included:

• A shift in the world's axis around the year 2000, leading to:
• Inundations of many coastal regions, caused by a drop in the landmass of about 30 feet (9.1 metres) combined with a melting of both polar ice caps, including :
• Southern England, leaving London as a coastal town
• The loss of much of Japan
• Flooding of northern Europe, which will happen very rapidly
• Open waters appearing where Greenland used to be

• New land appearing off the east coast of North America
• Widespread destruction in Los Angeles, San Francisco and the destruction of Manhattan and disappearance of New York
• Upheavals in both polar regions
• Volcanic eruptions in tropical regions and an increase in Pacific rim volcanic activity, especially affecting Japan (severe damage), China, parts of South East Asia, Eastern Australia, and the Pacific coast of South America
• A land bridge between South America and the Antarctic (as it used to be shown on the extraordinary old Piri Re'is maps).
• A general warming of currently cool areas, and cooling of warm areas.

Leo Taxil: The Great Hoaxer

In 1890s Paris, Gabriel Jogand-Pages, who also went under the pseudonym Leo Taxil, joined forces with a band of fellow "free thinkers" to indulge in a giant leg-pull against the Roman Catholic Church.

Jogand-Pages looked to the black arts to offend against the strong Catholic tradition of their country. This consummate confidence trickster was born in Provence in the mid 19th century, and educated in a Jesuit College. It was during his time here that he encountered Freemasonry, a forbidden subject in a Catholic boys' school.

Jogand-Poges became a Freemason, but then performed an apparent ideological about-turn by writing a denunciation of Freemasonry. In truth, Taxi's writings were little more than skilful hoaxes. He went on to guild the lily by inventing an ex-Satanist called Diana Vaughan, allegedly a descendant of English alchemist Thomas Vaughan, whom he dangled before a fascinated Catholic hierarchy as a potential convert. Diana, Taxil said, was a member of an organization called the Palladium, a worldwide Satanic cult reputedly run by Masons, acting under a man called Albert Pike, from Charleston in the USA. To give Diana some credibility, and a dash of devilish colour, Taxil even provided a pedigree for her and her fellow Satanists.

Part of this pedigree, and one of Taxil's greatest hoaxes, was the prediction of the birth and ancestry of the Antichrist (as mentioned in The Apocalypse of St John). One of the Palladium's priestesses, Sophia Walder, was presented as a literal "child of Satan", fathered by Lucifer. According to Taxil's prediction, Sophia would go to Jerusalem where in the summer of 1896 she would have intercourse with the Demon Bitru (or Sytry) and give birth to a daughter. Thirty-three years later this daughter would have a daughter by the demon Decarabia,

The diabolical Monsieur Taxil

The rituals of Taxil's Satanic cult were like the Masonic Rites of Mizraim

who after a further 33 years, in 1962, would give birth to the Antichrist.

The prophecy goes on to say that the Antichrist will make his mission public at the age of 33 in 1995. He will then bring about the Pope's conversion from Catholicism. This will be followed by a year of war which will result in the destruction of the Catholic Church and the conversion of many souls to the Antichrist.

Although the whole affair has been characterized as a hoax, there were a number of real elements. For example, Albert Pike was a very senior American Freemason who wrote a classic book on the subject (*Morals and Dogma of Freemasonry*), although there is no evidence that he was in anyway connected with Taxil's Satanic conspiracy.

The prediction also influenced the contemporary American psychic Jeane Dixon, who had a vision of the birth of the Antichrist somewhere in the Middle East on 6 February in the same year as Taxil had stated, 1962. In her vision, the parents of the child were the ancient Egyptian Queen Nefertiti and Pharaoh Akhnaton.

For symbolic reasons the Antichrist should be born in either Galilee or Jerusalem to balance the birth of the Christ. Nicholas Campion, who decided to draw up a nativity of the Antichrist, discovered that the day before there had been a solar eclipse.

Campion chose this time to draw up the Horoscope of the Antichrist, at 0:10am Greenwich Mean Time on 5 February 1962 in Jerusalem. At this time, in addition to the eclipse, all seven traditional planets – Mercury, Venus, Sun, Moon, Mars, Jupiter and Saturn – were in the sign of Aquarius,

THE ANTICHRIST

The Antichrist, when he arrives, will claim to be a god and will work miracles, such as raising the dead, walking on water, healing the sick, and possibly even flying like Simon Magus. The Jewish tradition has the incarnation of an evil power in a bald person with one eye bigger than the other and who is deaf in the right ear. Early Christians adopted the Jewish notion of a war between God and his adversary.

One historical person identified as the adversary was the Syrian king Antiochus IV Epiphanes (ruled 175–164 BC), who captured Jerusalem in 171 BC and used the Temple for sacrifices to pagan gods. He later ordered the persecution of the Jews recorded in the second Book of Maccabees.

The most famous Biblical reference to the Antichrist is in the Apocalypse of St John, chapter 13, although John does not use the actual term Antichrist, referring instead to a Beast.

Other identifications of the Antichrist have been Mohammed the prophet and both the Napoleonic emperors of France, a convenient term of abuse at a time of hostilities! Often the term Antichrist is applied by Protestants to the Pope (particularly Boniface VIII and John XXII), but this is a perversion of the original meaning. This is to be the opponent of, or false claimant of the throne of, the true Christ. The Antichrist is not to be confused with Satan: he is Satan's human representative on earth.

a rare astrological conjunction.

The vision of a child being born as Antichrist was taken up in 1976 by David Seltzer in his novel *The Omen*. Damien, obviously the Antichrist, grows up in the family of an American career diplomat. Several very popular films have been based on this premise.

Aleister Crowley, the 20th century's most notorious magician, includes a child character with specific magical abilities in his novel *Moonchild*. Although the novel does not mention the Antichrist, Crowley had obviously toyed with the idea of deliberately breeding a future Antichrist to complement his own self-assumed title of "The Great Beast 666".

Damien, the Antichrist from **Omen II**

The Dawning of Aquarius

Of all the dates and predictions examined in this book, the following timetable of dates is the most significant for the dawning of the Age of Aquarius.

Sixteenth-century fresco of Aquarius

Aquarius on a cigarette card of 1923

The following are the main contenders for the date of the dawning of the Age of Aquarius. These dates do not necessarily correspond with the arrival of the millennium, the Second Coming of Christ, or the Battle of Armageddon. They are an altogether gentler date with destiny, an ushering in of a period of earthly peace, not of Judgement, war in heaven, salvation and damnation.

1904 The beginning of the Aeon of Horus, as received by Aleister Crowley in April 1904 in Cairo. The arrival of this age was announced in The Book of the Law, the text of which was dictated to Crowley by the discarnate voice of Aiwass. This so-called "Aeon of the Crowned and Conquering Child" is often identified with the Age of Aquarius. For Crowley the new age spelled the end of the Christian period and its slave mentality.

1905 Entry to the Aquarian Age was identified by Gerald Massey as 2160 years after 255 BC. In fact, arithmetically it should have been calculated as 1906. The rationale for choosing 255 BC is also a bit doubtful, it being the date of the writing of the Septuagint, the Old Testament translated into Greek.

1911 Helena Petrovna Blavatsky's Theosophical Society chose this date on the basis of the words of the Lord Maitreya, as dictated to Krishnamurti, then Society's "World Teacher".

1914 Beginning of World War I.

1931 Messages received by Alice Bailey from Djwhal Khul, the discarnate Tibetan, indicated that the Age of Aquarius had begun.

1936 The beginning of the earth's axial shift as predicted by the American psychic Edgar Cayce.

1939 Beginning of World War II.

1943 Edgar Cayce stated that a new spiritual age would begin on this date.

1962 Birth of the Antichrist, according to both Leo Taxil (in the 1880s) and American clairvoyant Jeane Dixon (she reckoned the date as 6 February). Nicolas Campion chose 5 February, when all seven planets would be aligned in Aquarius. The Peruvian spiritual messenger Willaru Huayta, of the Quechua nation, also chose February 1962 as the commencement of the Age of Aquarius.

1963 Possible arrival of the Age of Aquarius, according to the author of *Liber Vaticinationem*. The beginning of the Hippie era, preaching the New Age of love.

1975 Arrival date for the Avatar of the New Age, according to the astrologer Dane Rudhyar.

1989 The break-up of Communism.

1995 Max Toth declares the arrival of the Kingdom of Spirit. The year in which Leo Taxil's Antichrist converts the Pope.

1997 The psychologist Carl Jung's date for the arrival of a New Age.

1999 Nostradamus predicts the arrival of the "King of Terror" in September, possibly followed by Armageddon – not really a candidate for the beginning of the New Age, but useful as a "marker". On 11 August 1999, there will occur the last eclipse of the 20th century, and a Grand Cross astrological formation.

2000 Chosen by many Christian and non-Christian prophets as the key date, including Nostradamus (the Second Coming), St Malachy (by inference), Edgar Cayce, the Virgin Mary at Fatima (by inference) and many Christian, particularly fundamentalist, writers and preachers; 4 or 5 May 2000 brings a significant astronomical

An Oriental depiction of Aquarius

formation which, according to Richard Kieninger and the Stelle group, will bring cataclysmic destruction.

2001 Arithmetically a more sound choice than the previous year, with support from the Seventh-Day Adventists, Hebrew chronology and Nostradamus. But both dates are more closely associated with the Apocalypse and Second Coming of Christ than the dawn of the Aquarian Age.

2010 A date favoured by a number of writers on esoteric subjects, including Nicholas Tereshchenko and Peter Lemesurier, the latter giving the French Institut Geographique Nationale as his authority.

2012 Jose Arguelles suggests that this year marks the end of a 396-year age, according to the ancient Mayan calendar. Terrence and Dennis McKenna regard the date as the culmination of many timescales.

2013 The end of the Inca calendar. According to Willaru Huayta, the New Age will be ushered in by the close passage to Earth of a huge asteroid.

2020 On 21 December this year Jupiter and Saturn will be in conjunction in Aquarius for the first time since AD 1404, according to Adrian Duncan. The ancient Jews certainly prized that particular conjunction as a portent of major changes.

2023 Woldben pinpoints this date as the beginning of the Age of Aquarius.

2060 Dane Rudhyar suggested that the Age of Pisces began in 100 BC, hence after the standard precessional period of 2160 years the Age of Aquarius will begin in either this or the following year.

2143 Christ's birth plus the precessional period of 2134 years, plus or

WHICH DATE IS RIGHT?

Everyone who has given an opinion on the likely date for the dawning of Aquarius seems to agree that it will be around the year 2000. This probably seems a bit vague, so let us see if we can narrow it down a bit.

It is reasonable to assume that the Age of Pisces started before Christ's birth, at the earliest around 200 BC. If we adopt the standard precessional period of 2160 years, the Age of Aquarius is likely to begin no earlier than 200 BC plus 2160 years or AD 1961. If we choose Christ's birth as the latest possible start to the Age of Pisces, then we get AD 2161 as the latest possible date for the dawning of the Age of Aquarius.

It is possible that the Age of Aquarius has already begun, in 1962 or 1963, and that the shackles of the old Age will now be completely thrown off until about 2001 or 2010.

minus a few years for inaccuracy about that particular birth date.

2160 Christ's birth plus the standard precessional period of 2160 years, also plus or minus a few years for the same inaccuracy; a date suggested by Woldben and Gordon Strachan.

2233 The earliest date for the Day of Judgement, according to the 15th-century monk Johannes Trithemius, and a possible time for the dawning of the New Age.

Hippies and the Age of Aquarius

Most people did not realize that there was such a thing as the Age of Aquarius until the hit musical Hair. *The astrologers had known about it long before.*

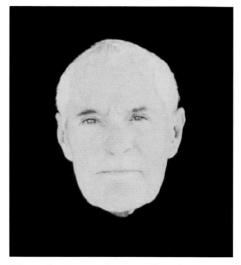

Timothy Leary, Harvard acid guru

Hair – *the era of love and enlightenment, or of sex, drugs and rock 'n' roll?*

First staged some 25 years ago, at the height of the hippie era, *Hair* celebrated in words and music the philosophy of turning on, tuning in and dropping out. The hippie movement popularized the notion of the Age of Aquarius, and perhaps saved humankind by doing so.

The world has still to catch up with this non-competitive, non-materialistic, non-violent view of life, although there are signs of a reawakening of interest in it. To many people the pace

of life has quickened considerably since those lazy, hazy days of the 1960s when the new message was "make love not war". Let us look at what has happened since those days of the acid culture.

The Vietnam War has largely been forgotten; the Cold War and Communism have faded away; the threat of the atomic bomb (so much part of hippie rhetoric) has receded; China is increasingly opening up to "market" values; and the sexual

revolution, having swung so far, is poised to crash back in the opposite direction. The LSD guru and ex-Harvard professor Timothy Leary, one of the leaders of the hippie movement, has, since his release from jail, made it up with Gordon Liddy (the agent who originally arrested him) and discovered the microcomputer. This device was originally assembled by two hippies on their kitchen table and programmed by Bill Gates, founder and owner of the Microsoft corporation and the richest dropout in the world.

Considering that their high point only lasted about five years, the hippies have had a great influence on the world. This has interesting implications for the Apocalypse. By tuning in to other "frequencies", be they drug-accessed or reached by mystical means, the hippies have helped to bring about a change in consciousness which may well have averted a different, darker destiny. This change may be seen in our present-day political leaders who generally have a more liberal attitude than many of their predecessors. It is possible, as is outlined in *Liber*

Vaticinionem, that certain key events force destiny to switch rails, as it were. The hippie movement may well have been one such event, averting a looming catastrophe.

The Age of Aquarius

There are many contenders for the date on which the Age of Aquarius started or is due to start, but everybody agrees that it is approximately the year AD 2000. (For the full astronomical background to the cycle of the Equinox through the Signs of the Zodiac, known as the precession of the Equinoxes, see Chapter 2.) All we need to know here is that the full cycle takes 25,725 years. Each sign takes one twelfth of this, or 2,143 years, although the figure has usually been taken as 2,160 years.

The sequence works backwards, almost as if the metaphorical "clutch" which controls the machinery of the universe has been "slipping" since the beginning of time. We are in the process of "slipping" from the Age of Pisces to the Age of Aquarius.

As we know the duration of the Age of Pisces, all we need is a start date to calculate its likely end. Most commentators have used the standard precessional period of 2160 years, but we can also apply the more accurate calculation of 2143 years.

Gerald Massey uses 255 BC as his starting point, and by adding 2160 years gets AD 1905, although it should have been AD 1906, because there are two year ones (1 BC and AD 1). A more obvious choice might have been Christ's birth, which would yield AD 2160 by the standard period, or perhaps AD 2143 as the date.

An Islamic interpretation of Aquarius

There is a second way of fixing the dawning of the Age of Aquarius, by choosing a date corresponding to some reputedly significant event, or to the reception of a particular revelation, the option taken by the majority of non-biblical end-time commentators. Aleister Crowley, for example, received *The Book of the Law* in Cairo in April 1904, and so for him the New Age began at that date. Details of other dates are to be found on pages 130-1.

The common thread that runs through most of these predictions is the arrival of an avatar, a reincarnation of a god, prophet or guru to guide humanity through the difficult transitional stage. There will certainly be a large number of false prophets appearing during the changeover period – in fact, that has been specified as being one of the signs of the times.

THE THREE AGES

Christianity is associated with Pisces, the sign of the fish, in a number of ways. For the first five to six hundred years of the Christian religion the sign most often associated with it was not the cross but the fish. The earliest disciples were fishermen. The symbol has taken on a whole new meaning with more recent and less orthodox practitioners of Christianity. The cult leader Moses David Begg, for example, used to encourage his female disciples to go "flirty-fishing", by which he meant securing converts to his cult by sexual means and seduction!

Before the Age of Pisces, from 2000 BC (in round terms) to Christ's birth, the sign of Aries, the Ram, prevailed. During this period many ram cults existed in the Middle East and elsewhere, and nomadic pastoral communities were common.

Prior to this, from 4000 to 2000 BC, Taurus the Bull held sway, and bull cults such as that of the Egyptian god Apis were prominent. Before the time coinciding with the sign of Taurus, civilization is lost to view, but the influence would have been from the sign of Gemini, symbolized by the Twins.

The Aetherius Society

Operation "Prayer Power", June 1979

One cold spring morning in 1954, after he had been experimenting with yoga trance states, George King heard a voice which told him to prepare himself to become the spokesman of the "Interplanetary Parliament".

In 1954, eight days after he had heard a mysterious voice telling him he had been chosen as the spokesman of the "Interplanetary Parliament", George King was "shaken to the core" by the miraculous appearance of a figure dressed in white robes and looking like an eastern saint. The apparition told him that he had been selected to act as the servant of the "Cosmic Masters". Thus the Aetherius Society was born, although King would not formally constitute it until 1960.

Soon King was holding public meetings. At these he would put on a pair of dark glasses and go into a trance to make contact with the communicating entity, often from Mars or Venus. Typically, the information passed through King would include movements of flying saucer fleets and also the advent of such terrestrial disasters as hurricanes and earthquakes. These upheavals in the natural world were thought to herald the new spiritual order which beings like the Master

Aetherius are attempting to bring to earth, very much in the manner of the Second Coming of Christ. (The Latin word Aetherius means "relating to the ether, or to the abodes of the gods".)

During one or two of the early public meetings held by King in 1955 the Master Aetherius mentioned that Jesus Christ was living on Venus, along with other religious leaders such as

Volcano on the surface of Venus, supposed abode of Christ

Buddha and Rama-Krishna. The Star of Bethlehem was said to be a flying saucer which had brought Jesus to earth for his first incarnation. Press ridicule ensured sell-out performances.

On 23 July 1958 King claimed to have met with the avatar of Jesus Christ on Holdstone Down, in the west of England. As a result of this meeting, King made a practice of visiting the "high places" of the world and charging them with spiritual energy.

Courses offered by the Society, which is also incorporated as a church, include spiritual healing and yoga. Its rationale centres on the continuing mental transmissions from extraterrestrial sources to the Society's founder, and the concept of being able to store spiritual energy for later release.

George King believes that we have missed the Apocalypse by a hair's breadth several times recently, and have been saved by the spiritual battle he and others like him are waging on our behalf. During these battles, members of the Aetherius Society bear arms in the form of spiritual energy, which they generate through, among other things, prayer. King, who holds degrees from the Theological Seminary at Van Nuys in California, has invented a spiritual accumulator based on crystals and gold, into which he claims he can store the energy of thousands of hours of prayer, to be released during times of spiritual crisis.

Venus, with its overtones of love, holds a special place in the cosmology of the Aetherians. It is from the spiritual counterpart of this planet that they expect the imminent arrival of an avatar, perhaps a returning Jesus Christ or the Buddha as Maitreya.

OTHER FLYING-SAUCER MESSAGES

The 1950s saw a change in the type of communication experienced by mediums. Long used solely (or so it seemed in the public imagination) as conduits for messages from the dead, mediums began to receive information from flying saucers or UFOs (unidentified flying objects). These messages are in the main no less banal and sketchy than those received from the spirit world.

The "School of Universal Philosophy and Healing", run by Gladys Spearman-Cook in London, used regularly to deliver hints of an impending "Interplanetary Brotherhood". Also in London, the White Eagle Lodge, a spiritualist group in South Kensington, devoted most of its energies to making contact with flying saucers, although reporting little of interest to the average uncommitted spectator.

UFOs became a vogue in the world of spiritualism and even the movement's official magazine, *Psychic News*, began to devote a lot of space to reporting major saucer sightings.

In America, too, contact with beings from space tended to eclipse for a while spiritualism's principal concern of reaching the spirits of the dead. "Summerland", the name given to the realm inhabited by spirit life, was even relocated by some to another planet in our galaxy. Even major Christian cults were bitten by the UFO bug – the Mormons, for example, allocated other planets as post-Apocalypse repositories for unredeemed souls. Into their post-Judgement Day "Telestial Kingdom" will go all people who have been "unclean", such as liars, adulterers, sorcerers, and those who have broken the covenants.

A UFO or flying saucer – a new messenger of the gods

Manson's Apocalypse

The hippie era was not all love and peace: there was a sinister side to it as well. Charles Manson wanted to release the horrors of the pit.

Charles Manson

Charles Manson, once described as a "hippie car-thief cult-leader sex-maniac bastard butcher", and his "family" of some 20 girl members (called Satan's slaves) plus sundry hangers-on established a headquarters at a ranch near Death Valley in California in the late 1960s. Manson had once been a member of the Scientology cult, whose techniques, he thought, would enable him to do, or be, anything he wanted.

From early 1961, Manson began to prepare for the end of Western civilization which, he was convinced, was about to be destroyed by some sort of Armageddon. He became obsessed with the idea of hastening the arrival of this catastrophe. One way of lending it a hand, he thought, would be to provoke a race war. He talked a great deal about the blacks he had met in prison who had secret arms caches, to be used at some future time against their white neighbours. One of Manson's strategies for starting a race war owed a lot to the occult: the beaming of "hate vibes" into the troubled black ghetto of Watts.

Another way of undermining American society would be to begin a campaign of murder. It is these murders, especially that of actress Sharon Tate, wife of director Roman Polanski, for which he is remembered. Manson's aim was to kill the famous, but the not so famous were also caught up in his plan. How many were murdered by "the family" is still not known.

Manson's hate-fear-sex-death commune was governed by a collage of myths drawn from Scientology, the Process Church of the Final

Film director Roman Polanski with his wife Sharon Tate

Judgement, the Solar Lodge of Aleister Crowley's OTO and Beatlemania. For his "theology" he drew on obscure interpretations of the lyrics of the Beatles' songs (see panel), and the Apocalypse of St John.

Manson derived some of his key ideas from the Process, whose publications included *Satan on War*, *Jehovah on War*, *Lucifer on War* and a magazine devoted to peddling ideas of fear and death. The leader of that cult, Robert Sylvester DeGrimston Moor, claimed to be a reincarnation of Christ (as did Manson at a later date), while his wife, Mary MacLean, said she was a reincarnation of Hecate, goddess of magic, ghosts and witchcraft. In March 1974 the publishers of Ed Sanders' book on Manson, *The Family*, fought a court case over the extent to which the Process had influenced Manson: the Process lost.

Manson's followers were encouraged to drink animal blood, hate blacks and believe in the idea of "race war Armageddon". This would erupt in 1969 after Manson and the "family" had lit the touchpaper by committing murders which would be blamed on blacks. Once wholesale slaughter had got underway, his group would slip away to an underground paradise. (Manson borrowed this concept from the American Cyrus "Koresh" Teed, whose ideas inspired the hollow-earth theory of the Nazis.) According to Manson, this paradise would be available at the right time, when the "seven holes on seven planes" came into alignment. The "family" would then "squirt through to the other side of the universe" via the "Hole" which would open up near their desert hideaway.

WHAT THE BEATLES NEVER INTENDED

Manson read personal messages into the Beatles' song lyrics. Even an innocuous detail like the all-white cover of one of their albums was interpreted as a sign of an impending race war. One of the Beatles's songs, Helter Skelter, he took to signify his mission and the rush towards Armageddon. For the English Beatles, helter-skelter meant simply a children's slide in an amusement park! Manson saw the Beatles as four of the angels of the Apocalypse (8:7–12). Blackbird, he took, of course, to be a racial reference. The song Sexie Sadie thrilled one of his "slaves", Susan Atkins, who was also known as Sadie Mae Glutz.

For Manson, Revolution 9 was both revolution and the ninth chapter of "Revelation", in which St John says "in those days shall men seek death, and shall not find it; and shall desire to die, and death shall flee them". Generous-hearted as ever, Manson proposed to help such people. More obvious song titles, like Happiness is a Warm Gun, were taken literally. The song Piggies may well have inspired the murder of a plump middle-aged couple with a carving knife and fork.

On several occasions Manson tried to telephone the Beatles to discuss his paranoid fantasies. Mercifully for them, he never got through.

Charles Manson was an avid reader of the Bible, that vast repository of hidden apocalyptic messages. He annotated his copy of the Apocalypse of St John, drawing parallels between it and his life with the "family". The dune buggies they used were the horses of Helter Skelter with "breastplates of fire" (chapter 9). One of Manson's favourite passages from 9:21 was "neither repent they of their murders, nor of their sorceries, nor of their fornication, nor of their thefts". What better justification for his way of life?

He saw himself as the angel of the bottomless pit who will at the appointed time pass with his family through the Hole to his kingdom, and from there emerge every so often, like locusts, to ravage and harry mankind.

The angel with whom Manson identified was called Abaddon in Hebrew, Apollyon in Greek (meaning "destroyer"), and in Latin Exterminans, the Exterminating Angel.

Armageddon did not arrive on cue: instead, on 15 October 1969, police rounded up the remnants of his "band of nude and long-haired thieves" and put them on trial. Manson, together with his main disciples, Patricia Krenwinkel, Susan Atkins and Leslie Van Houten, was convicted of the Tate-LaBianca murders and jailed for life.

Manson said: "I am not the King of the Jews nor am I a hippie cult leader. I am what you have made of me . . . In my mind's eye my thoughts light fires in your cities." If he had his way, the Apocalypse would arrive tomorrow.

The Great Wars

Wars have been the subject of many prophecies down through the ages. The French Revolution was predicted by many prophets, at least 20 of them from the 15th and 16th centuries, including Nostradamus.

British artillery in action in the "war to end all wars" – Battle of the Somme, 1916

During the early 20th century many prophets foretold World War I as the "war to end all wars", although most of them settled on 1913 rather than 1914 as the date it would start. In Germany the years 1911 to 1913 were referred to in popular parlance as *glutjahr*, *flutjahr* and *blutjahr*; that is to say, the year of fire or heat (1911), the year of flood (1912) and the year of blood (1913).

The last of these was perhaps selected for cyclical reasons, because it was exactly a century since Prussia declared war on France, Napoleon was victorious at Lützen, Austria declared war on France, Wellington defeated the French at Vitoria, and Napoleon was defeated at the "Battle of Nations" at Leipzig: 1813 was a good "blood year", indeed.

One little-known prophet, Rudolf Mewes, a physicist, published in 1896 a book in which he predicted conflict between Eurasian and Asiatic countries, beginning in 1904, which corresponds neatly to the war between Russia and Japan (1904–5). The complicated system he devised for making his predictions was based on meteorological fluctuations. Although fallible, this system is of interest today because of the light it might shed on the increasingly wild fluctuations in climate we face in the last decade of this century.

From his observations of fluctuations in the earth's magnetic field, of sunspots and of the intensity of the aurora, or northern lights, Mewes developed the idea of a cycle of 111.3 years. Each cycle, he deduced from his investigations of the time span 2400 BC to AD 2100, experiences two periods of war and two periods of advances in the sciences and the arts. Each of these periods, or sub-cycles, lasts about 27.8 years.

Mewes' efforts were, by and large, way off target, but they did encourage others to try to develop a theory along similar lines. A system of prophecy that could predict just about everything, from the quality of harvests to

Battle of Leipzig, the Napoleonic War

the cyclical fluctuations of economies and the stock markets and the timing of the Apocalypse, would be no mean achievement.

Perhaps the oldest theory of cycles applied to the timing of the First World War is the Egyptian Sirius cycle of 1461 years. If we count back 1461 years from the dates of the First World War (1914–18), we get 453–457, a time when imperial Rome was under attack by the Germanic tribes. If we use the same cycle to count back from World War II, we fall only a little short of AD 476, a date widely given for the ending of the Western Roman Empire, when the emperor Romulus Augustus was deposed by the Goths under Odoacer.

The Sirius cycle is too long to be of use in predicting future wars. The historian Arnold Toynbee (1889–1975) tried to work out a shorter peace-war cycle by analysing history back to 1495. He came up with four "regular cycles", each of which had a "prelude" (sometimes with a premonitory war), a "general war" (for which read pan-European war), a "breathing space", a "supplementary war" and, finally, a "general peace".

The four cycles were 1568–1672, 1672–1792, 1792–1914, and 1914 until 2118 or 2036. According to this system, we are currently in a period of "general peace". Unfortunately, Toynbee's four cycles are of uneven length and so will not work as an adequate prophetic dating system, but the principle of alternating periods of peace and war might well tie up with some underlying cycle. If we could discover this underlying cycle, then perhaps we should know the date of the last of all wars, Armageddon.

THE WORLD'S HEARTBEAT OR BIOLOGICAL CYCLES

Known biological cycles like heartbeat, menstruation, tides, sunspots and the orbits of planets have always suggested that there may be other as yet unknown cycles. Astrology has since time immemorial tried to relate one set of known cycles, the planetary movements, to the affairs of men. Such horoscopes are still thought by some to be able to plot recurrent events in an individual's life, as well as personality tendencies. The study of the three biorhythms is almost as popular as horoscopes.

One well-known cycle is the Metonic cycle, which demonstrates that every 19 years the phases of the moon coincide exactly with the calendar date. The Metonic cycle was discovered by the Greek astronomer Meton in around 432 BC.

Edward Dewey has catalogued almost every known phenomena with the potential for varying cyclically over time. He has discovered, for example, that the breeding cycles of several species of wild animals, such as foxes and wolves in Canada, increases to a maximum every 9.6 years. This in turn is explained by a similar cycle to be found in the fluctuation of rabbit-fever, and hence of food supplies for the predators concerned. Dewey has also tried to find other connecting cycles upon which to base useful conclusions.

Weather cycles are partially dependent upon the differential heating of the earth's surface, but so far meteorologists do not seem to be able to come up with an reliable set of predictive relationships.

Biological cycles govern sleeping and waking

The EARTH STRIKES BACK

Will the long suffering Earth
finally grow tired of having her riches
plundered and precipitate the prophecies
of the Apocalypse in a way that the
original prophet could not even have
guessed at?

Earthquakes in Divers Places

When St Mark asked Christ (13:8) by what signs His Second Coming would be signalled, the Lord said "There shall be earthquakes in divers places, and there shall be famines and troubles."

Earthquakes, famines and troubles have always been with us, but there has certainly been an increase in earthquake activity over the last decade.

In the Old Testament the earthquake was one of Jehovah's traditional means of showing disapproval. Isaiah (29:6) records that the doomed city of Ariel "shalt be visited of the Lord of hosts with thunder, and with earthquake, and great noise . . . and the flame of devouring fire".

The earthquake is a basic natural phenomenon against which man has little defence, except perhaps prediction. Earthquake belts are so extensive that a concerted upheaval could destroy most of the Pacific rim, southern Europe, the Near East and Southeast Asia. Even Britain is not immune, having had an earthquake registering 5.2 on the Richter scale as recently as 1990.

In recent years earthquakes have been occurring in previously stable areas. Liaoning province in Manchuria, for example, had not had a major earthquake for 100 years before 4 February 1975. The quake registered 4.8 on the Richter scale – a logarithmic measure of energy, which means that each step up the scale represents a tenfold increase.

Shortly before the earthquake, animals in the Liaoning area began to behave strangely. Andrew Robinson describes it: "Snakes awoke from hibernation prematurely and lay frozen in the snow; rats appeared in groups so agitated that they did not

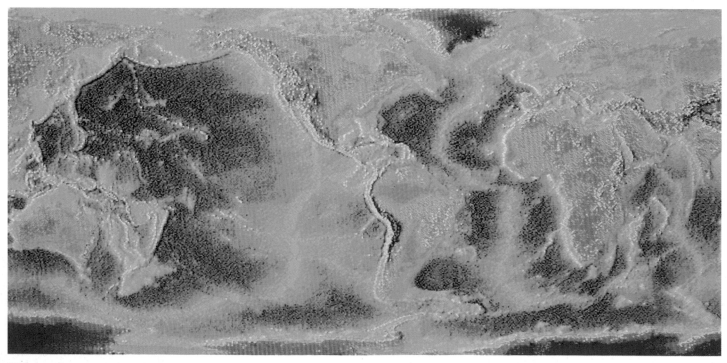

The Earth is ringed with shifting tectonic plates which constantly grind against each other

fear human beings; small pigs chewed off their tails and ate them".

When the earthquake struck, sheets of light flashed in the sky, jets of water and sand shot into the air, bridges buckled, and the majority of buildings in the main towns of the province were wrecked. Only 300 people died because the populace received plenty of warning.

The greatest chronicled loss of life due to an earthquake occurred in July 1201 in the Near East and the Mediterranean. Almost every city in the area was affected and the human toll was estimated at 1,100,000. The highest death toll from an earthquake in modern times occurred at T'ang-shan in China (7.9 on the Richter scale) on 28 July 1976, when between 500,000 and 750,000 people perished.

The world's most destructive earthquake in material terms occurred on the Kanto Plain, Japan, on 1 September 1923 (Richter scale 8.2). This annihilated two-thirds of Tokyo and four-fifths of Yokohama and caused the sea floor of the adjoining bay area to drop an amazing 1300 feet (400 metres).

A major earthquake in Tokyo now would have other serious consequences, as it would provoke worldwide Japanese disinvestment, causing a worldwide financial crisis as Japanese insurance companies and businesses strove to rebuild the country.

The increase in earthquake activity observed over the last two decades may indicate that our time-ride to the end of the millennium is set to become even bumpier. Recent quakes of 6.7 on the Richter scale on the India/Nepalese border have been eclipsed by the more recent 8.5 Richter scale quake in

CALIFORNIA PREDICTIONS

The famous 1906 earthquake in San Francisco demolished almost five square miles (13 sq km) of the city and was accompanied by a huge rupture 270 miles (430 km) long. The San Andreas fault system – 60 miles (96 km) wide and 800 miles (1280 km) long – and its associated systems continues to generate tremors, and the whole shifts on average about 1–1½ inches (2.5–3 cm) a year.

In October 1989 there was

California – threatened by destruction

another serious earthquake along the San Andreas fault (6.9 on the Richter scale), which, in addition to killing nearly 300 people and damaging many buildings, caused a freeway and a section of the Bay Bridge linking San Francisco with Oakland to collapse. The quake was followed by a massive fire in the Oakland hills, and another quake in January 1994.

Such devastation must have reminded Californians of the predictions of Edgar Cayce. He had predicted destruction and minor earth disturbances from 1980 to 1990 as a preliminary to much greater destruction that will occur in Los Angeles and San Francisco in the last decade of the millennium.

Nostradamus appears to have prophesied earthquakes for Nice, Monaco, Rheims, Pisa, Genoa, Savona, Siena, Capua, Modena and Malta (X:60). A very specific earthquake for "Mortara" and the sinking of part of England is quite specifically prophesied in IX:31. Nostradamus's reference to an earthquake in California is not clear, except that it will occur in May.

Hokkaido in Japan, which resulted in massive tidal waves.

Some observers are convinced that the number of earthquakes has roughly doubled in each of the decades since 1950. The side effects of future earthquakes might include nuclear spillage, as some Eastern European reactors have been built along fault lines.

Conventional wisdom has it that earthquakes are caused by friction between the vast "tectonic plates" supporting the continents. An alternative view is that their incidence is related to sunspot activity, and sunspots might well have some bearing on the configuration of the planets in the solar system.

Comets in Collision

The Russian scientist Immanuel Velikovsky (1895–1979) was born in the small town of Vitebsk in 1895. The son of a Hebrew scholar and publisher, he was vividly aware of the disaster and catastrophe stories in the Old Testament.

Velikovsky – 20th-century polymath

Velikovksy was a physician and psychologist who had studied at both the Medvednikov Gymnasium in Moscow, where he graduated with distinction, and at the universities of Moscow and Edinburgh. He then went to work in Berlin, where he became one of the founders of Scripta Universitatis. Here he met Albert Einstein, who was in charge of the organization's physics publishing programme.

In the 1930s Velikovsky went to Vienna to study psychoanalysis and the ideas of Sigmund Freud. It was at this time that he first became interested in ancient civilizations. The idea for his first and probably greatest book, *Worlds in Collision*, was born here. In this he wrote about the momentous natural phenomenon which had once devastated the world. The major ancient civilizations, including the Greeks, Samoans, American Indians, Chinese, Egyptians and Hebrews had left accounts of this cataclysmic event, which Velikovsky believed had been caused by a comet. He started putting

Venus – planet of love or rogue comet, bearded star and feathered serpent?

together the pieces of evidence offered by the ancient scribes, and eventually reached the conclusion that it must have happened 3500 years ago.

The Bible gives one of the symptoms of the event as the Sun standing still in the sky. This Velikovsky dated to 1450 BC. Other cultures, on the other side of the world, recorded an enormously long night, the obverse of the experience noted in the Middle East – the same event seen from different sides of the earth. Velikovsky interpreted this as the approach of a huge comet, which had the effect of temporarily slowing down the Earth's axial rotation.

Velikovsky maintained that during a 52-year period from around 1502 BC to 1450 BC the Earth had been struck twice by the tail of this enormous comet, which had erupted from Jupiter, the largest planet in the solar system. These collisions had caused tidal waves, earthquakes and volcanic eruptions which radically altered the geography of the planet.

As a result, maybe whole continents like Atlantis sank into the ocean while new landmasses were raised from the sea bed. The sky rained fire, noxious gases, and millions of white-hot rock and tektite fragments. The two poles may even have reversed or at least fluctuated in position.

The comet, declared Velikovsky, threatened the stability of Mars as it passed before finally becoming the planet we know today as Venus. Venus would be extremely hot, he said, owing to its recent life as a comet, and it would have high concentrations of hydrocarbons in its atmosphere and a disturbed rotation. These notions were

to be verified by space probes decades after Velikovsky's pronouncements.

Velikovsky predicted correctly that the Moon would have strong magnetic activity, that its surface would have a carbide and aromatic hydrocarbon content, and that Jupiter would be found to give out strong radio emissions.

You can imagine the furore his ideas caused in scientific circles. How could this be, they all cried. The establishment tried to block the publication of his work, but Velikovsky outsmarted his critics by allowing mass-market publications like *Readers Digest* and *Harpers* to publish his findings in America, thus assuring widespread awareness of his theories.

Some scientists still do not fully accept his ideas, despite the accuracy of many of his predictions. If we were visited by a huge comet in 1500 BC and again in 1450 BC, as has been recorded in many holy books, and as Velikovsky believed, what is to prevent a similar "second coming" by a destructive natural phenomenon from space in 2000 AD?

THE BIRTH OF VENUS

The ancients described the planet Venus as an intensely bright body, and ranked it second only in importance to the Sun and the Moon. Today it is just a small speck in the sky. Velikovsky believed that Venus erupted into life with spectacular results, an event recorded by many ancient civilizations.

The Aztecs called Venus "the star that smoked" and Quetzalcoatl ("the Feathered Serpent"). Their holy books record how at one time "the sun refused to show itself and during four days the world was deprived of light. Then a great star appeared; it was given the name Quetzalcoatl . . . [and] a great number of people . . . died of famine and pestilence."

The Greeks tell of how Phaeton (the "blazing star") nearly destroyed the world by fire, and then was transformed into Venus. The Jewish *Talmud* describes its comet-like appearance as "fire hanging down from the planet Venus", while the

Aztec gods provide corroboration

Midrash describes the "brilliant light of Venus blazing from one end of the cosmos to the other". The Assyrians called Venus "the fearful dragon . . . who is clothed in fire".

In China, at the time of the Emperor Yao, "the sun during a span of ten days did not set" and "a brilliant star issued from the constellation Yin", demonstrating gravitational effect on the Earth during the birth of Venus.

Changing Magnetic Fields

Our view of the solar system is gradually progressing away from the unchanging perfect rotating sphere studded with stars envisaged by the ancients to one of an altogether more dynamic and less stable system.

The planet's orbits and axes can, it seems, be affected by a whole range of other bodies moving randomly through the solar system.

Changes in climate have been observed to coincide with changes in the Earth's magnetic field. The nature of the relationship is not known, but the sudden extinction of whole species of animals – dinosaurs are a good example – may have coincided with abrupt changes in the Earth's magnetic field. These changes have now been proved (see panel).

Now, if these magnetic changes sound comfortably far away in time, think again. Researchers have found compelling evidence in the ashes from Australian Aboriginal camp fires that the North and South poles were in very different positions from where they are today. Indeed, a complete reversal of the poles is indicated. The changes of magnetic direction and their associated upheavals have taken place relatively recently.

A sudden reversal of magnetic poles, as has happened in the past, would cause both serious earthquakes along existing tectonic fault lines and huge tidal waves, generated by movements of the ocean floor. It would then be easy to imagine sinking islands, flooded coastal areas and low-lying inland areas, and even some ocean floors rising clear of the waterline. Many areas would experience flooding every bit as total as the one that taxed Noah's ingenuity. Predictions of such events by prophets like Edgar Cayce have been dismissed, but in view of this new evidence they should perhaps be reconsidered.

If the Earth were to tilt suddenly the planet would be swept by hurricanes and tidal waves. There is evidence to support the notion that such cataclysmic changes have occurred in the past. The extensive coal deposits in Britain are a good indication that in the Carboniferous era when the deposits formed the region was tropical, with extensive fern forests and swamps. Large areas of North America were similarly covered in rainforest. By contrast, western parts of Australia and southern Africa were buried under tons of ice.

One possible explanation, offered by Alfred Wegener in the 1920s, is of continental drift, but this presupposes that large land masses have "drifted" thousands of miles from their original positions. With the "axis flip" scenario it seems plausible that herds of mammoths

A dramatic shift in the magnetic poles would change the face of the world

were happily grazing in a warm Siberia until one fateful day the climate changed. The freeze was so rapid as to render the meat of the mammoths trapped in the ice still edible and even palatable after long periods of time. One mammoth was found to have undigested flowers in its stomach. A contrary view is that mammoths were always Arctic dwellers, but this seems unlikely. Such a harsh environment would surely not have provided enough vegetation for them to grow so large.

Experiments with gyroscopes (fast-spinning flywheels mounted on spindles) show that, given the right impetus, they will flip over and then quickly resume a new stable rotational position. The Earth could be viewed as a gyroscopic-type system, which requires the impetus of a large passing body – such as Venus or an asteroid – to give it the necessary gravitational impetus to tilt over.

An electrical engineer called Hugh Brown suggested in 1967 that the Earth's axis tilted through 90 degrees as recently as 7000 years ago. Brown's idea of regular polar shifts seems improbable, but the occasional cataclysmic axial flip is very much in the realm of the possible.

One advocate of Brown's theory, Adam Barber, predicted in a pamphlet – optimistically entitled *The Coming Disaster Worse than the H-Bomb* – that a 135-degree flip would occur in the next 50 years, at least before 2005. Fortunately, this prediction can be taken with a rather large grain of salt, but writings on the subject by Peter Warlow, published in the *Journal of Physics* in 1978, deserve to be taken more seriously.

The Earth's magnetic fields

Warlow puts the sudden axial flip at 180 degrees; that is, the North and South poles actually swap places. He successfully demonstrated this with a model, and backed it up with sound calculations. The flip occurs once roughly every 2000 years, he thinks.

Like Velikovsky, Warlow takes the evidence of myths very seriously. He claims that the Egyptians recorded four separate such swaps, during which the Sun appeared to reverse its motion across the sky. The most recent of them occurred, so he says, in 700 BC and again in 1500 BC, the latter corresponding to Velikovsky's dating and to the destruction of the Minoan civilization in Crete.

THE MAGNETIC PROOF

The geological record shows that the Earth's magnetic field has periodically reversed, with disastrous consequences for most living things, including man.

The geological record of these total polarity reverses is preserved in molten rock which has cooled at different periods in geological time. Every time such a rock solidifies it preserves a weak magnetic field induced by the Earth's gravitational field. Active volcanoes producing newly cooled lava and even man-made objects, like cooling pig iron, will take up the same weak field.

Even fireplaces will, in the course of heating and cooling, gather to themselves this weak field. Work has been done on both Australian Aboriginal and pre-Roman English fireplaces to catalogue the condition of the Earth's magnetic field at specified historic times.

Geologists have studied the ocean floor around the spreading mid-ocean ridges and have discovered a series of bands of rock which have solidified at different times, the furthest from the ridge being the oldest in geological time. Reading these bands, geologists discovered that the Earth's field has reversed more than 20 times in the strata so far sampled. The last flip, or reversal, apparently lasted only for 2000 years.

Even over a short period in recent history a degree of wandering of the north magnetic pole has been identified. In the early 17th century magnets pointed 11 degrees east of north. By 1643 they pointed 4 degrees east of north, and by the 1650s they had temporarily returned to due north.

Plagues and the Black Death

A virulent new strain of cholera emerges in India, and an outbreak of diphtheria breaks out in ex-Soviet Russia.

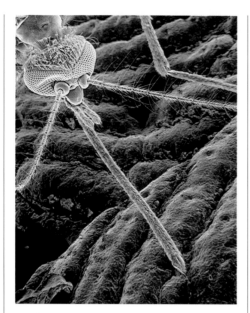

Malaria is again on the increase

Recent outbreaks of deadly diseases confirm a growing trend that has been worrying scientists for the last decade. It is slowly dawning that the triumph of medical science over disease is no longer as inevitable as it seemed back in the 1950s. The bugs are fighting back, most worryingly by becoming drug-resistant.

Evolution works for bugs, too: the hardiest specimens are the ones that survive. Tuberculosis, which kills 3 million people a year worldwide, is beginning to acquire antibiotic resistance. In the USA a dangerous alliance has been formed between AIDS and tuberculosis. Another former scourge, malaria, is now making a comeback, claiming 2 million deaths per year worldwide. The fight against it is being hampered by both the drug-resistance of the microscopic parasite that causes the disease and by pesticide-resistance in the mosquitoes that carry it.

This has been partly countered by an acceleration in drug research and the production of even stronger drugs

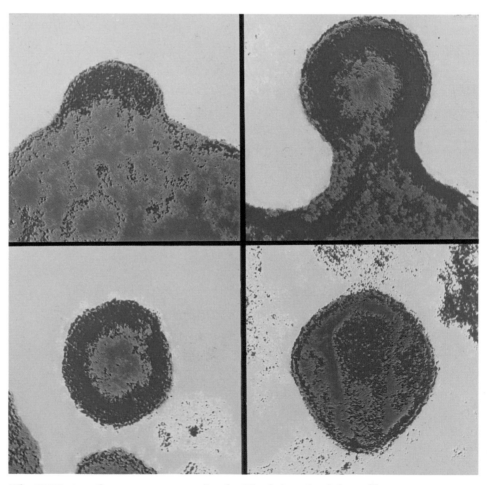

The HIV virus has yet to prove to be the Black Death of the millennium

to deal with each new threat. But drugs are not winning the race, and even in industrialized countries thousands of people are dying every year from antibiotic-resistant infections which they pick up in hospital while receiving treatment for less serious conditions.

Man's intrusion into the tropical rainforests has exposed him to new reservoirs of infection from animals and insects which are further taxing the ingenuity of the scientists. Several of these apparently "new" diseases are probably caused by old monkey viruses, including AIDS, Ebola and Marburg fever. However, if you thought that you were only at risk from such diseases in tropical regions, think again. In the eastern USA the rapid increase of Lyme disease is due primarily to new housing developments being built close to wooded areas, as the bacteria responsible are carried by mice and deer, their normal hosts.

New farming and food processing procedures also put us at risk from bacteria and viruses. While often hygienic in the accepted sense of the word, these processes provide exotic mixing vessels for new infections. Recent salmonella and listeria scares in the UK, Europe and North America have arisen from intensive breeding of hens in batteries, a procedure which did not exist on a large scale until the 1960s.

The food industry's practice of using every last piece of slaughtered animal has meant that unwholesome remains now re-enter the food chain as food for another animal. Recent outbreaks of "mad cow disease" have been caused by this practice, the brains of infected

An infection kills cows and cannibals

THE BLACK DEATH

The Black Death, or bubonic plague, has still not been completely eradicated, although outbreaks are now rare and deaths few. It first appeared in Europe during the reign of the Roman emperor Justinian, in AD 542, and in the Middle Ages accounted for millions of deaths as it ravaged the continent repeatedly. With each successive epidemic it lessened in severity as people built up immunity to it, so that by the 20th century it became almost confined to warmer climates.

One of the few recorded outbreaks of the disease in Western Europe in the 20th century occurred in the 1920s in England. Workmen engaged upon building a railway cutting near Lewes, in Sussex, unwittingly dug into an old plague pit, undisturbed for centuries. Before long the men began to succumb to an illness which was initially diagnosed as pneumonia. Several of the workmen died before the authorities realized that they were dealing with something a great deal more sinister and hastily quarantined everyone in danger. Eventually the crisis was brought under control, but it is sobering to realize that the seeds of death in the form of plague bacteria can survive in the soil for centuries.

animals being recycled and fed to cattle. This would never normally occur in nature; left to their own devices, cows would not eat meat. The only parallel may be found in New Guinea, where the transmission of Creutzfeld-Jakob's Disease was traced to the cannibalistic practice of one person eating the infected brains of another.

Genetic mutation by bacteria and viruses can produce new "super" germs. Dangerous strains of influenza have been found in south China, where integrated pig and duck farming is practised. The food interdependence of these two types of animals has produced a "genetic mixing vessel" which is recombining different flu viruses to form new and more virulent types.

Many viruses can undergo genetic change at frightening speed in response to environmental conditions. As a result of this "genetic forcing house", some very unpleasant new viruses and bacteria have come into existence. The coincidence of a few factors favourable to them could lead to an epidemic of appalling proportions. Consider AIDS: suppose that instead of transmission by body fluids this disease passed from one person to another via aerial infection, in the same way as influenza. The arrival of something as transmissible as influenza and as virulent as some of the viruses introduced from new "gene pools" or from animals could make the Black Death or the 1918 flu pandemic, which claimed millions of lives in Europe, seem mild.

It would be natural justice if the Apocalypse arrived not from the heavens but from the soil and forests that man has been systematically destroying: a case of the Earth striking back!

Nature Meets the Supernatural

An ancient apocalyptic theme is assuming new prominence as the 20th century winds down to its end: the accelerating destruction of the environment.

Lunar phenomena such as this eclipse have always been considered portentous

Nuclear accidents, oil spills, global warming, vanishing forests, rapid desertification of vast areas of Africa, the greenhouse effect, damage to the ozone layer, the sighting of comets and meteors, the arrival of new plagues and the distortion of usual climatic patterns – all these bring to mind similar environmental happenings and motifs written about in the Bible.

The Apocalypse of St John speaks of the breaking of the seven seals. The first four seals released the well-known four Horsemen of the Apocalypse, plague, famine, war and death (6:1–8). The fifth seal revealed saints and martyrs. The sixth seal revealed natural and ecological disasters (6:12–9:2): "And, lo, there was a great earthquake; and the sun became black as sackcloth of hair, and the moon became as blood". The sky and sun sometimes show strange lighting effects before an earthquake, and the moon taking a bloody cast has always been considered an omen as well as being a symptom of natural disaster.

Possibly a fall of great comets or meteors is indicated in "the stars of heaven fell unto the earth, even as a fig tree casteth her untimely figs, when she is shaken of a mighty wind" (6:13). The shaking might refer to a wobbling of the Earth's axis, which is likely to accompany the arrival of these destructive heavenly bodies.

With the destruction of the ozone layer which "departed as a scroll when it is rolled together" humankind will be forced to seek shelter wherever it can find it. The next verse (6:15) tells how at that awful time everyone, from kings and rich men down to ordinary free men, will hide "themselves in the dens and in the rocks of the mountains". In the recent past this verse was interpreted as the population escaping nuclear fallout in underground shelters. With such a possibility receding, it might be more appropriate to read this as some ecological disaster.

In the next chapter St John sees in his vision "four angels standing on the four corners of the earth, holding the four winds of the earth, that the wind should not blow on the earth, nor on the sea, nor on any tree". This verse conjures up an eerie vision of a silent land with not a breath of wind, that pregnant pause before disaster strikes.

Before the full horrific forces of destruction are released, a voice commands that the servants of God be identified by a mark on their foreheads so that they can escape harm. Interestingly, the same marking is carried out by the Beast, so that he, like God, will be able to recognize his own.

Until this is done, the avenging angels are instructed to "hurt not the earth, neither the sea, nor the trees" (7:3). It is almost a direct plea to our age to cease raping the earth, polluting the sea, and cutting down the once great forests of the Amazon.

Finally, after the seventh seal has been opened, there is a period of silence before "there were voices, and thunderings, and lightnings, and an earthquake" (8:5). The earthquake precedes widespread volcanic eruptions from which fire, hail and blood rain down on the vegetation. Then a "great mountain burning with fire" (8:8) turns the sea to a blood colour, poisoning one-third of the fish in the ocean.

The third trumpet brings yet greater destruction, "and there fell a great star

San Francisco suffers an earthquake

from heaven, burning as it were a lamp, and it fell upon the third part of the rivers, and upon the fountains of waters". The star is named Wormwood, which does not appear in any

catalogue of stars. The word is used as a pun on the bitter herb which went into the making of the drink absinthe, "and the third part of the waters became wormwood; and many men died of the waters, because they were made bitter" (9:10–11) or poisonous.

This might indicate a poisoning of water supplies, perhaps by some new plague from outer space. Another ambiguous passage concerns a type of poisonous locust which is sent to plague mankind (see panel).

When the fourth trumpet sounds more cosmic changes occur, reminiscent of Velikovsky's theories of cosmic cataclysm: "the third part of the sun was smitten, and the third part of the moon, and the third part of the stars; so as the third part of them was darkened, and the day shone not for a third part, and the night likewise" (8:12).

This ends the passages in the Apocalypse of St John which can be read as having ecological significance.

SUPERNATURAL LOCUSTS

The fifth trumpet provokes a strange race of creatures to emerge from the fires of the volcanoes, "there came out of the smoke locusts upon the earth"(9:3). These locusts were commanded to kill men who were not protected by the seal of God upon their foreheads. They were to kill with stinging tails like scorpions, but their victims were to die slowly over five months. These locusts sound more like demons than animals. They are described as being like horses decked with armour; they had the faces of man, and wore, or

looked as if they wore, iron breastplates, with gold crowns on their heads. They could be looked upon as demons from the bowels of the earth, perhaps even from Hell itself.

It is not impossible, though, that they were as natural as the volcanoes from which they sprang, being some kind of creature whose bite provokes illness and finally death after five months of suffering. As locusts were very familiar creatures to the authors of the Bible, it seems strange to use the word for anything other than some kind of flying insect.

Apocalyptic Weather

In the first three years of the 1990s world weather has been distinctly weird. In one 12-month period alone the three most damaging climatic disasters in US history occurred.

Hurricane Diana limbers up for a bout of destruction in September 1984

In September 1992, Hurricane Andrew devastated Florida. Then, in March 1993, a giant blizzard swept from Florida to Maine. The US National Weather Service called it "the single biggest storm of the century", because it released more snow, hail, rain and sleet than any other US storm since 1888. The relentless rain brought floods to the American Midwest, wreaking damage that may, in dollar terms, make it the costliest weather disaster of all time.

The director of the Weather Service, Albert Friday, wondered if these events actually indicated not just a shift in the weather, but a more dramatic shift in the climate. There have always been natural disasters, but the number witnessed in recent years is verging on the apocalyptic. Even storms in southeastern Spain, which did not make the world news, turned the sky a sombre green, flushed the bats from their normal habitat, and resulted in the region of Murcia being declared a disaster zone.

Tropical cyclones, variously called typhoons (in the East) or hurricanes (in the West), are among the most powerful and destructive earthly phenomena known to man, capable of travelling at terrific speeds (up to 200mph/316km/h) and covering vast areas (up to 580 sq miles/1500 sq km). Fortunately, as hurricanes form over the sea, meteorologists usually have time to forecast their moves, and quite often they blow themselves out before reaching land.

In September 1989 Hurricane Hugo crossed the eastern seaboard of the USA at a breath-taking maximum speed of 160mph (260km/h), killing 71 people and causing $10 billion worth of damage. At peak strength such a wind can release energy that is equivalent to 25 Hiroshima-type hydrogen bombs.

In August 1992 Hurricane Andrew swept across Florida, causing $16 billion worth of damage in and around Miami. It was one of the most expensive natural disasters in recorded history. Every year as many as 50 cyclones rage through the tropics, but seldom do they hit such heavily populated areas. Thunderstorms kill more people in the USA than any other natural phenomenon.

On the other side of the Atlantic, on 16 October 1987, the south of Britain awoke to find a landscape devastated by a freak storm, which disrupted lines of communication and blocked many routes into the capital. The London Stock Exchange was forced to close down early as a result of the difficulties. Winds were stronger than any experienced in southern Britain in the previous 200 years, with gusts exceeding 80mph (130km/h). More than 19 million trees were uprooted in just a few hours, some falling on iron railings with such force that the spikes were driven deep into the timber.

All this took place despite a forecast of mild weather issued by the Meteorological Office only hours before the storm hit southern Britain (see panel). The total financial cost of this natural disaster was £1.5 billion ($2.2 billion).

On the next day of financial trading, Monday 19 October 1987, a crisis of another sort struck when almost all of the world's stock markets went into virtual free-fall. More value was wiped off stock prices in that week than had been lost in the stock market crash of

MODERN WEATHER PROPHETS

Modern-day meteorologists, though they are equipped with the most up-to-date information technology, seem to be no more accurate in their predictions than their entrail-reading predecessors.

Meteorologists and astrologers have a great deal in common. Both have a long history of using precise observations and tables as the basic tools of interpretation, and in both professions that added bit of intuitive flair is still required to interpret the chart and draw the right and relevant conclusions from the mass of confusing data thrown up.

British meteorologists certainly drew the wrong conclusions from the chart for the night of 16 October 1987. Likewise, modern astrologers, even with the aid of computer-produced charts, can be way off target with their predictions. By contrast, the Elizabethan astrologer Simon Foreman could predict the day of his death without so much as a pocket calculator to help him.

Supercomputers can still be wrong

For many centuries, meteorology was in fact the step-child of astrology. The greatest thinkers of antiquity regarded it as self-evident that weather conditions were governed by the stars. Thinking in this area may yet come full circle when the relationship linking conditions active in the solar system, such as sunspots, and atmospheric conditions are better understood.

1929 during the same period of time. Were the two events connected? Had some mysterious, unknown cycle reached its crescendo, both on the physical plane and in that vast psychological arena which determines the prices of stocks and shares?

An even stronger, but not so widely publicized, wind hit Britain in January 1990, on Burns' Day (named after the Scottish poet Robert Burns), when daytime winds reached a furious

107mph (173km/h) and claimed a toll of at least 47 lives.

These and other disasters have piled one on top of another in such a short period of time that the world's main insurance market, Lloyds, has been brought to its financial knees by the sheer weight of claims. In the coming decade we may have to face increasingly vicious and destructive natural phenomena as the climatic system continues to destabilize.

Hell on Earth: Volcanoes

Volcanoes are perhaps the natural phenomena which bear the closest resemblance to Hell in man's imagination. A computer file of active volcanoes compiled between 1950 and 1975 listed no fewer than 700.

By 1981, the computer file of potentially active volcanoes listed over 1300 of them. Volcanoes are destructive enough in themselves, but there is an even more insidious side to them.

On 27 August 1883, the Indonesian island of Krakatoa literally blew itself up as a result of volcanic activity, killing more than 36,000 people and spewing tons of pumice into the atmosphere. So much of this material was released that the heat from the Sun was not able to reach the Earth's surface, and temperatures around the world were significantly lowered for many months.

That was the effect of just one volcano! A succession of such explosions could rapidly precipitate a chain reaction. Minute rock particles with glassy fragments, pumice, superheated steam and sulphuric acid drops can spread amazingly quickly over large areas. (In 1982, El Chichon in Mexico spread a veil of 20 million tonnes of sulphuric acid droplets around the world in less than a month.)

It may take months for the dust and rock particles to finally settle out of the atmosphere, but the sulphuric acid droplets can ride the winds for years. The resultant "dust-veils" cause beautiful sunsets and strange optical effects, like the blue moon reminiscent of St Mark's words about the Apocalypse: "the sun shall be darkened, and the moon shall not give her light" (13:24).

Reduced temperatures on Earth might trigger other apocalyptic effects. The extra gases, sulphuric acid and dust particles belched out into the atmosphere by these eruptions would reduce the atmospheric temperature sufficiently to give the CFCs (chlorofluorocarbons) the catalyst they have been waiting for, enabling them to commence a wholesale "slaughter" of the ozone layer.

If this scenario comes to pass, then Armageddon will look tame by comparison. The Earth's ecosystem is delicately balanced. The onset of excessive volcanic activity would greatly increase the depletion of the ozone layer, leading to a fall in crop yields and a horrendous rise in skin cancers and burns.

The Apocalypse of St John does not use the word volcano, but nevertheless has some pretty accurate descriptions

Volcanoes are the physical embodiment of the conventional vision of Hell

Dust from Krakatoa blocks the sun

of phenomena that we would recognize as volcanoes. These are called upon by the angels in the last days to help destroy mankind. The angels are commanded to sound seven trumpets, the first of which ushers in a firestorm, "hail and fire mingled with blood, and they were cast upon the earth: and the third part of trees was burnt up, and all green grass was burnt up" (8:7). Such a firestorm has got to be the fruit of widespread volcanic eruptions.

The destruction continues with the second trumpet, "and as it were a great mountain burning with fire was cast into the sea: and the third part of the sea became blood; and the third part of the creatures which were in the sea, and had life, died; and the third part of the ships were destroyed" (8:8–9). This passage is reminiscent of the eruption of Vesuvius in AD 79, when those who were rowing away from the quay at Herculaneum were destroyed.

The fifth trumpet provokes a strange mixture of natural and supernatural disasters for man, "and there arose a smoke out of the pit, as the smoke of a great furnace; and the sun and the air were darkened by reason of the smoke of the pit." (9:3). From this fiery pit there emerges a strange locust-type creature.

St John would seem to have been under no illusions that volcanoes would be called upon by God's angels to destroy mankind.

DESTRUCTION OF ATLANTIS

Probably the most violent volcanic explosion in ancient times occurred on the Aegean island of Santorini (or Thera), 70 miles (113 km) north of Crete, in c. 1645 BC. It was probably the largest volcanic explosion known to man. Santorini today consists of three islands. These lie round a great expanse of water marking the huge caldera, or crater, where Santorini used to be before the volcanic explosion. Two volcanic islets are now at the centre of the water. The younger of these is still intermittently active.

The eruption began with an explosion which shot a column of debris 20 miles (30 km) high and scattered it over the whole of the eastern Mediterranean. When sea water finally entered the huge crater, it quickly turned to steam, exploding with unimaginable force and sending thousands of cubic miles of steam and fragmented lava into the air.

The crater measures about 7 miles (11 km) from north to south and close to 5 miles (8 km) from east to west, an area of 35 square miles (90 sq km) and reaching a depth of up to half a mile. The volume of rock displaced is estimated at about 14–16 cubic miles (60–65 cu km), an unimaginably enormous quantity which would have been pulverised, melted and even vaporized by the force of the blast.

It has been suggested that this monumental blast destroyed the civilization of "Atlantis" in nearby Minoan Crete. If such a place had indeed existed, it would have been covered with ash and pumice within a few hours. The tidal wave generated by the massive explosion would have wrecked the coastline of Crete and even reached up to Knossus, "sinking" Atlantis. If this is so, then it ended an entire civilization of considerable complexity. Such an explosion could also wipe out a modern civilization.

Santorini: destroyer of Atlantis?

Bombs from Heaven: Meteors

A meteor may strike at any moment – the miracle is that it has not happened many times before. The solar system contains many bodies that could wreak havoc on Earth.

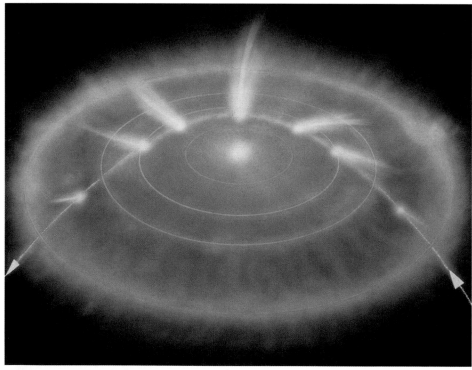

Halley's Comet, one of the few well-documented comets

An apocalyptic event took place in Siberia in the early morning of 30 June 1908. An eye witness of the terrifying occurrence recounts:

"When I sat down to have my breakfast beside my plough, I heard sudden bangs, as if from gunfire. My horse fell to its knees. From the north side above the forest a flame shot up.

Then I saw that the fir forest had been bent over by the wind, and I thought of a hurricane. I seized hold of my plough with both hands so that it would not be carried away. The wind was so strong it carried soil from the surface of the ground, and then the hurricane drove a wall of water up the Angora [River]."

The farmer and his horse were more than 125 miles (201 km) from where the disaster struck. The farmer had felt the effects of a great natural phenomenon: a meteorite hitting the Earth. A rock the size of four or five supertankers ploughing into the Earth at a speed some 40 times faster than a bullet, and white hot from passing through the atmosphere, can cause as much damage as a huge nuclear bomb.

If this meteor had hit a large city rather than the Siberian wilderness, it would have destroyed it along with all life. One late-20th-century seer has actually predicted this very fate for London in the year 1999 – a chilling thought indeed.

Let us consider another "if". What if the meteor were the size of one of the larger asteroids (over 400 miles/650 km wide) which travel in very erratic orbits through our solar system? Might not such a mammoth meteor wipe out most of civilization as we know it? Far fetched? Certainly not to that farmer whose breakfast was so rudely interrupted, nor to the souls who were in its path, and so did not survive to give their testimony.

Scientists from Dartmouth College, New Hampshire, writing in *Nature* magazine, claim that Chixculub in Mexico is the impact point of a meteor which exterminated the dinosaurs. Whether this is true or not, a massive crater more than 120 miles (190 km) wide can be caused by a meteorite only several miles wide.

The impact at Chixculub threw up dust and debris with such force that particles have been found 1000 miles (1600 km) away in Haiti. Scientists reckon that the resulting worldwide cooling caused by the screen of dust and debris in the atmosphere might well have wiped out the dinosaurs. Man, despite technology, is probably less resilient than the dinosaurs were, and would succumb rapidly to the major climatic shift that would be caused by such a phenomenon.

According to Willaru Huayta, a Peruvian descendant of the Quechua nation, 2013 will mark the end of the current Inca calendar. In this year he predicts that a huge asteroid will pass close to the Earth's orbit, and will cause by its gravitational field a number of catastrophes. He states that the meteor will be three times larger than Jupiter. Interestingly, Jupiter is often implicated in terrestrial disasters, possibly because of its size. When this asteroid has spun away from the Earth's orbit and the resultant cataclysms have subsided, what remains of mankind will, according to Huayta, become a "seed" people, in the same way that Noah's children allegedly repopulated the Earth. These people will be the new Adam and Eve and the basis of the "sixth generation" as defined by the Incas. This event is well

A meteorite – a bomb from Heaven

WARNINGS FROM THE ASTEROID BELT

The asteroid belt between Mars and Jupiter (at right edge)

The asteroid belt is a group of fragments (some larger than 400 miles/ 644 km across) which orbits the Sun between the paths of Jupiter and Mars. Some of these monsters, which can exceed 400 miles (650 km) in width, have very irregular paths. Astronomers have yet to work out these out, but they known not to follow regular ellipses round the Sun.

Asteroids are thought to be the remains of a tenth planet which exploded at some time in the past. According to Dr David Hughes of Sheffield, England, there are perhaps 100,000 "small" asteroids floating around in the solar system that we cannot detect because of their size. He defines "small" as about $3^3/_4$ miles (6 km) across. They are important because a glancing blow by an asteroid this size would produce a crater large enough to swallow two average-size cities.

within the bounds of possibility, and would give a concrete meaning to the idea of a New Age.

Even a concentrated shower of much smaller meteorites striking a heavily populated area could cause more immediate damage than a concerted nuclear strike. Just imagine the damage if our protective atmospheric skin were to be thinned out as a result of this, with its concomitant

temperature drop plus increase in ultraviolet and cosmic radiation.

Apart from a few well-known exceptions, like Halley's Comet, no one knows how to predict the paths of a fraction of the meteors passing through the solar system. Even Halley's Comet did not show up quite as brightly as predicted the last time it passed Earth in the 1980s. So who can say what is hurtling towards us?

ACKNOWLEDGEMENTS

The publishers would like to thank the following sources for their kind permission to reproduce the pictures in this book:

Ancient Art & Architecture Collection; Andes Press Agency; Bettmann: UPI; **Bridgeman Art Library:** Agnew & Sons/London, Bible Society/London, British Library/London, British Museum/London, Carnavalet Museum/Paris, Cecil Higgins Art Gallery, Bedford, Conde Museum/Chantilly, Christie's/London, Crozatier Museum/Le Puy en Velay, Giraudon, Huntingdon Library & Art Gallery/San Marino, Index, Kunsthistorisches Museum/Vienna, Lambeth Palace Library/London, The Louvre/Paris, Versailles Museum/Paris, National Gallery/London, Pitti Palace/Florence, Pierpont Morgan Library/New York, Prado/Madrid, San Marco Dell'Angelico Museum, Florence, Tate Gallery/London, Uffizi Gallery/Florence, Vatican Library/Rome, Victoria & Albert Museum/London, City of York Art Gallery/York; **ET Archive:** British Museum/London, Terry Engel Gallery; **Mary Evans Picture Library; Ronald Grant Photo Library; Sally and Richard Greenhill; Hulton Deutsch Collection; Images Colour Library; Peter Newark Pictures; Popperfoto; Rex Features:** Action Press, Archetti, Brooker, Globe, LGI, Photo Associates, Prisma, SIPA, Stills, Today; **Science Photo Library:** Anderson, NASA, Julian Baum, Sally Bensusen, John Bova, Dr. Fred Espenak, David Hardy, Hank Morgan, NASA, NOAO, George Post, Rev.Ronald Royer, Roger Ressmeyer, Gregory Sams, Sheila Terry; **Tony Stone Worldwide:** Anthony Cassidy, Chris Harvey, Hugh Sitton, James Strachan, John Turner, John Warden, John Wyand.

Special thanks are also due to Lily Richards at The Bridgeman Art Library, Christina Morgan at The Mary Evans Picture Library, Dermot Kavanagh at Rex Features and Andrew Simmen at The Science Photo Library.